ROUTLEDGE LIBRARY EDITIONS:
SOCIOLOGY OF EDUCATION

I0121735

Volume 46

TEACHING UNDER ATTACK

TEACHING UNDER ATTACK

WALTER ROY

R Routledge
Taylor & Francis Group

LONDON AND NEW YORK

First published in 1983 by Croom Helm Ltd

This edition first published in 2017
by Routledge
2 Park Square, Milton Park, Abingdon, Oxon OX14 4RN

and by Routledge
711 Third Avenue, New York, NY 10017

*Routledge is an imprint of the Taylor & Francis Group, an informa
business*

British Library Cataloguing in Publication Data
A catalogue record for this book is available from the British Library

ISBN: 978-0-415-78834-2 (Set)
ISBN: 978-1-315-20949-4 (Set) (ebk)
ISBN: 978-0-415-79251-6 (Volume 46) (hbk)
ISBN: 978-0-415-79252-3 (Volume 46) (pbk)

Publisher's Note
The publisher has gone to great lengths to ensure the quality of this
reprint but points out that some imperfections in the original copies
may be apparent.

Disclaimer
The publisher has made every effort to trace copyright holders and
would welcome correspondence from those they have been unable to
trace.

TEACHING UNDER ATTACK

Walter Roy

CROOM HELM
London & Canberra

© 1983 Walter Roy
Croom Helm Ltd, Provident House, Burrell Row,
Beckenham, Kent BR3 1AT

British Library Cataloguing in Publication Data

Roy, Walter
    Teaching under attack.
    1. Educational sociology – Great Britain
    2. Education and the State – Great Britain
    I. Title
    370'.19'0941   LC191.8.G7

ISBN 0-7099-2212-4
ISBN 0-7099-2213-2 Pbk

Typeset by Mayhew Typesetting, Bristol
Printed and bound in Great Britain by
Biddles Ltd, Guildford and King's Lynn

CONTENTS

INTRODUCTION

At the beginning of the 1980s, the teaching profession has to work in an increasingly hostile environment. Successive cuts in educational expenditure, imposed by governments and local authorities, coinciding with falling rolls, have produced a scarcity of jobs, both in primary and secondary schools, and mounting teacher unemployment. Those who have jobs feel less and less secure; conditions of service are worsening and prospects for promotion seem poor. Such circumstances reflect the downgrading of the whole education service which has been a feature throughout the 1970s and is likely to get worse in the next few years.

Politicians argue that the country's economic state is such that education cuts, and loss of teachers' jobs, are inevitable; fewer children mean fewer teachers, and the schools must bear their share of the economic rigours facing the nation. If the attacks on education were confined to its material fabric, one could argue the case for greater investment on economic grounds: better education should produce better qualified and more enlightened citizens to cope with the enormous problems facing the country with unemployment now well beyond three millions and affecting nearly a third of all school leavers; the decline of an economy based largely on manufacturing and service industries outdated in the electronic age; the change in the age composition of the population with more and more old people needing care and attention; the growth of deprivation and the social problems often created by the breakdown of the family unit, with loneliness and sickness affecting tens of thousands. Beyond our own problems there are the global challenges of world hunger and the ultimate threat that the human race may destroy itself. However, what is happening goes beyond the struggle for resources between conflicting interests in society. The attack on teaching, in particular, has its roots in a philosophy resting on the belief that it is central government, its ministers and civil servants, that must determine not only the shape of the school system, but of the curriculum, and the methodology of the teaching process. Teachers must therefore be subordinated to a political will based on the notion that only an all powerful state knows what is best for its citizens; the individual counts for less and less because the assertion and the development of individuality, which is an essential

1

task of the education process in a free society, gets in the way of political aspirations and systems which require both uniformity and conformity. Powerful politicians thus see the teacher of the future essentially as a communication machine, teaching to a centrally designed and, if necessary, centrally dictated curriculum with standards of attainment monitored by a government department. The accountability of the teaching profession for what it does is, under such a system, replaced by controls removing from the teacher the professional freedom to shape the curriculum to meet the needs of the children he knows, and to use methods best suited to local circumstances.

The purpose of this book is to describe both the nature and the direction of the attack on teaching, and to provide constructive proposals for meeting it. The first two chapters analyse the challenge to the teaching profession and describe the political context in which the battle for resources takes place. The following three chapters examine the part played by the teachers' union, with particular emphasis on activities of the National Union of Teachers, the largest and most powerful association of teachers in this country; teachers' pay and conditions of service are reviewed in some detail, as are both the problems of and the possibilities for promotion. The remainder of the book examines the issue of accountability and considers the essence of professionalism − what makes a good teacher and a good school. The book concludes that the outstanding need for teachers is to answer the attack on the profession by enhancing their own professionalism, to resist the encroachment of politics on the teaching process, and to promote the essential harmony rather than controversy, which schools and children need.

As a member of the Executive of the National Union of Teachers, and the Chairman of its Education Committee, I write as a committed, but not uncritical member of a great professional association, itself under attack. I am indebted to the members, officials and officers of the NUT for providing essential information, though the opinions stated are, of course, my own and neither the NUT, nor anyone else bears any responsibility for them. Other sources have been used and are acknowledged as appropriate, but most of what is written is based on personal experience as a teacher and headmaster over a quarter of a century. I am grateful to Nancy Harrison, my indefatigable secretary, for typing the manuscript, to my wife for reading it, and last, but not least, to my colleagues in a great profession.

Walter Roy

1 THE CHALLENGE TO THE TEACHING PROFESSION

At the beginning of the 1980s, the education service faces a new dark age; school closures, both in cities and in villages, are the order of the day, with no regard for the quality of life in the areas affected or the wishes of the parents. The report of the Department of Education and Science for 1981 shows that twice as many schools were closed in 1981 than in the previous year.[1] Successive expenditure cuts have produced a depressing state of affairs in thousands of schools: tattered textbooks shared by more and more classes of children; shortages of essential equipment affecting the quality of teaching in all types of schools; worn out furniture, with no hope of replacement; shabby buildings in need of repair and redecoration, but still holding thousands of oversized classes. The evidence of this deterioration comes neither from the protests of thousands of teachers, who could be said to have a vested interest, nor from the numerous reports of parents organising themselves up and down the country to fight school closures and the educational cuts affecting schools in all areas of the country, but from the carefully researched and cautiously worded reports of Her Majesty's Inspectors,[2] to be discussed in the next chapter. What has happened in the late 1970s and early 1980s has put the right of every child in Britain to a decent and free education, enshrined in the 1944 Education Act, at risk.

And what of the teachers themselves? Thousands of them, trained at the nation's expense, qualified graduates, aching to get into schools to teach, are either unemployed, or doing jobs, if they are fortunate, totally unconnected with their chosen vocation. Those who leave university training departments and colleges of education fill in scores of application forms for an ever decreasing number of teaching posts, emerging deflated and demoralised from the occasional interview which raises hope, only to find that others who have made the shortlist have been trying for even longer. The cherished vision of an earlier teacher generation, to create a graduate teaching force, with appropriate qualifications to meet the challenges of the twentieth century, is gone. Yet alongside this desperate situation, schools are crying out for teachers of mathematics, of the sciences, of modern languages, of the craft subjects: no retraining programmes worthy of the name have got off the ground, and half the colleges of education in the country have ceased to exist within the last decade, standing empty and desolate, with no hope of redemption. Those who are fortunate to have posts are feeling less and less secure as the threat of unemployment grows with each economy wave: 40,000 teaching jobs, including 25,000 compulsory redundancies, are likely to go by September, 1983[3] if the government's latest expenditure reductions take place in the form envisaged. Attempts to sack teachers, made in Barking, Avon, Trafford, Oxfordshire and Staffordshire, have to be met by weapons repugnant to the teachers of Britain — confrontation, industrial action of one sort or another, and finally, as in Barking, by a teacher's strike.[4]

But alongside the attack on the material fabric of the education service, there is a more dangerous, and far-reaching attack on the profession itself: the freedom of the teacher to do his job in the best interests of the children, using curricular patterns and methods most appropriate to his circumstances, free from political interference and petty tyranny, is itself under threat, a threat which represents the greatest challenge to the teaching profession since the introduction of state education in 1870. This is a three-pronged attack: first, coming from central government, seeking to centralise the curriculum, and removing not only from teachers, but from local education authorities, the real say of what is taught in our schools; second, from the advocates of testing and monitoring programmes, particularly from the government's Assessment and Performance Unit,[5] who see in the battle cry for higher standards of literacy and numeracy an opportunity to enhance the validity of its testing procedures at the expense of teachers' judgments. Last, but not least, the profession is under attack from politicians, who have power and patronage in a system using confidential reports which affect the whole process of appointments and promotions.[6] The immediate need is for teachers to fight for the children's as well as their own, interests, and this makes it essential for them to understand clearly both the nature and the direction of the attack, and above all, to take it seriously.

How has all this happened and why is teaching under attack? It could all too easily be argued that the economic state of the nation is such that a reduction in public expenditure is inevitable, and that education cannot escape its share of retrenchment in a recession. Whichever government is in power, cuts in educational expenditure would therefore happen, even though they may vary in their extent and intensity; it is certainly true that both the Labour Government of the late 1970s, under James Callaghan as Prime Minister, and the

Conservative Government of Mrs Thatcher, in office since 1979, are both on record as having imposed cuts on the education service. At first sight, major differences appear to exist between the two major political parties. The Labour Party is certainly opposed to the vicious cuts which the Conservatives have made, and are making, in the education budget; and on the issue of comprehensive education, the consensus which existed earlier in many areas, has been replaced by renewed controversy; attempts by Conservative politicians to reintroduce the 'eleven-plus' type of selection procedures, to re-establish selective schools,[7] to give public money, through the assisted places scheme, to 'academic' independent schools, have met with strong opposition from the Labour party, which continues to stand for the comprehensive school, which is also supported by the new Social Democratic Party and the Liberals.

But whereas Conservative and Labour politicians may differ passionately about the issue of comprehensive schools, there are increasing and alarming signs that on other major issues, the differences are more apparent than real, and are likely to lessen in the 1980s. Both the last Labour and the present Conservative Government have imposed severe cuts on educational expenditure; the cuts made by the present administration are more vicious, but those in control of both parties clearly accept the need, as they see it, to reduce public expenditure, including that on education. However, given some differences of policy in resource allocation, with labour conceding more resources to the education service, the common ground between both parties is seen most clearly in a philosophy based on interventionism in the work of schools. Details of what the curriculum should be, and how schools should organise their work, are spelt out with increasing fervour and clamour by successive Ministers and ex-Ministers, whether Labour or Conservative. The new Social Democratic Party's educational blue print[8] spells out interesting and, for teachers, hopeful ideas: resistance to pressure on primary schools to be under-resourced as rolls fall; access to 'some form of facilities' for the under fives, with local education authorities producing a definite plan for their education; the determination to introduce legislation to end selective secondary schooling in those areas still refusing to introduce comprehensive schools; teacher training to be extended from three to four years. There are plans to end the GCE 'A' level examination and reform the tertiary curriculum, to revive a strengthened and reconstructed Schools Council, and double the spending on books, stationery and equipment. Of all recent party political pronouncements, it seems the most forward looking and positive, with sufficient far-sightedness and courage to tackle thorny issues and bearing the unmistakable touch of Shirley Williams, Secretary of State for Education and Science in the last Labour government, who, whatever her critics may say, had a real feeling for the needs of children. But the SDP is of course, untried in government.

In the meantime, many politicians of whatever party, display an unmistakable attitude, that they, and only they, know what is best for the nations' schools, and that the teachers exist to carry out their will. The German philosopher Hegel saw the state as 'the march of God upon earth'; it is an apt description of the way some of our political masters approach anything to do with the schools. The language used may be less crude, but the intention is the same: the schools exist to serve the interests of society as interpreted by those who hold political power and the purse strings, and the teachers who need to be made to toe the line. As they see it, the curriculum must conform to a pattern required by a society whose norms are materialism, competition, and the needs of manufacturing industry. The spectre that this opens up for the twenty-first century is frightening; a centrally dictated curriculum taught by the smallest number of teachers possible – the teacher being the communication machine.

There are, of course, many politicians, and civil servants at the Department of Education and Science and certainly the inspectorate, who resist such a notion. They maintain, with the teachers, that there is value in maintaining the essence of professional freedom, but expect teachers to be sensitive to a changing social and political climate which requires a modification of an attitude that the teacher is usually, if not always, right. There is room for a constructive dialogue between the professionals and the politicians, and hopefully, the emergence of a new consensus.

The early pioneers of state education who succeeded in putting the first Education Act of 1870 on the statute book had the vision to see the need for, and acknowledge the right of, every child to go to a school provided by the state, serving the needs of a local community. Both the need and the right are challenged by those politicians who see education as a commodity to be bought and sold; in its extreme form, this can amount to a policy of demolishing the state education system as such, as is the intention of the advocates of the educational voucher scheme: both Sir Keith Joseph and Dr Rhodes Boyson are said to favour some variations of such a scheme, and it is not at all unlikely that it may yet find its way into Conservative Party educational policy. An attempt to introduce such a scheme was made in Ashford, Kent, in 1979, and could be the model of things to come if its advocates have their way.

The scheme of issuing parents with such vouchers was invented some 20 years ago by Milton Friedman, the great exponent of a monetary policy supposed to solve all ills in society. Parents are given a voucher, whose value is equal to the cost of schooling for their child for a given period, usually a year; parents then choose a school and present their offspring plus voucher to their favoured institution, private or public; the school's income is determined entirely by the number of vouchers presented; these can be redeemed from a central body or the local education authority. Thus 'good schools' become popular and flourish, and 'bad schools' fail to attract pupils and go to the wall; the mechanism of the market place determines supply and demand, and consequently the numbers of teachers employed, the accommodation available and the curriculum provided.

A large scale experiment with educational vouchers was introduced in 1971 in Alun Rock, California, with some federal monetary aid. Although considerable claims were made for its success, it was abandoned after five years. But the idea proved sufficiently attractive to the politicians controlling the Kent County Council to commission a feasibility study in 1976, and to encourage the formation of a national pressure group appropriately named 'FEVER' 'Friends of Educational Voucher Experiment' in selected regions; there is indeed something feverish about the activities of the advocates of vouchers – the fantasy of a purely commercial competitive scheme determining the number, size and quality of schools – the children are seen as the raw material, to be haggled over like second-hand clothes in a third-rate junk shop. Dr Rhodes Boyson, Parliamentary Secretary to the Department of Education and Science, and a former secondary headmaster, is on record as a powerful advocate[9] of the voucher scheme, although he qualified his support by admitting that some parents would be disappointed and unable to get their first choice of schools.

However, the feasibility study commissioned by the Kent County Council concluded that the scheme would be both costly and unworkable; first, the study made it clear that popular schools would soon become oversubscribed; as demand increased, some schools would expand, requiring additional accommodation quickly, which would inevitably have to be of a temporary nature; other schools, less popular, would have available good facilities, which would stand unused. One cannot move laboratories at a moment's notice, and playing fields cannot be shifted at all. Nor do the advocates of the voucher scheme seriously consider the effects of such changes on the teaching force.

The greatest asset any school can have is a highly professional, proficient and able staff. Voucher schemes are a sure recipe for insecurity of tenure, and the destruction of morale among the teachers. Nor does one find all 'good' teachers in one school and all 'bad' ones in another. Not only bad, but good teachers in undersubscribed schools would therefore soon lose their jobs. Furthermore, the cost of introducing vouchers into the Ashford area of Kent alone, was estimated at between £600,000 and £1 million per year.

Even with such indisputable facts staring them in the face, arising from the feasibility study commissioned by themselves, Kent County Council still decided to press ahead with the scheme. The major teachers' organisations, led by the National Union of Teachers all opposed it, the NUT setting out its reason in a well argued pamphlet 'The Future at Risk'. The then Secretary of State, Mrs Shirley Williams, expressed her total opposition, but the present Conservative administration continues to be attracted by the idea. In Ashford itself, only 10 per cent of the parents said that they would choose different schools from the ones at present attended by their children. The attempt to introduce educational vouchers is a typical politically inspired move — it has no roots in any demand made by the community, is not based on popular support, and is the worst kind of political dogma besetting the educational scene.

Attempts to destroy schools and to alter the fundamental principles of providing a free education still have to stand the test of carrying public opinion; some are so flagrant that this proves impossible. But other attacks on teaching are more sophisticated, and are presented in a way likely to command considerable support. The attacks on the teacher's freedom to exercise professional judgment for the benefit of the pupils in his care are clearly evident in the periodic attempts made by government to move towards greater control of the curriculum. The political double talk which, in one breath, disclaims any such intention, whilst at the same time pursuing the objectives with vigour, is plain to all who take the trouble to review the events leading to the present alarming situation.

The roots of the attack on the teachers' freedom — itself one of the best guarantees of the democratic process in a free nation — go beyond the 'Great Debate' to be described in the next pages. The immediate post-war period was marked by enthusiasm for education; the 1944 Education Act, with its provision for better opportunities and free education for all children, gave rise to a tremendous school building programme; the founding of scores of new universities, the institution of a system of free grants for higher education all characterised the optimism of the post-war years; somehow, the money for educational expansion was found in a Britain scarred by war, with its cities in need of rebuilding, with food rationing continuing into the post-war era, and a tremendous war debt hanging round its neck. And yet, resources were made available as an unparalleled programme of education expansion took off the ground in the 1940s and 1950s, because there was the political will to do it, and the popular support for it. Those who claim that Britain in the 1980s cannot afford to spend more on education would do well to remember what a poorer and partly destroyed country managed to achieve some 35 years ago. But, as equality of educational opportunity became a reality, the defenders of the old privileges, and believers in separatism in our school system took fright, and soon determined to show their opposition. It came in the shape of the 'Black Papers', attacking supposedly low academic standards in the comprehensive schools, attempting to prove that standards of literacy and numeracy were declining, and that behaviour and morals in the new secondary schools were worsening. With interest in education greater than ever, politicians of both parties soon realised that the education process lent itself to controversy; where there was none, it could be created by the political process; education thus became a live issue in the party political battle.

Politicians thrive on controversy and it was not surprising that alongside issues which were genuinely controversial, such as the reorganisation of secondary education, other issues were raised which, in themselves, were generally considered to be outside the field of party politics. One of these related to the nature of the curriculum; another to the standards of attainment in schools; neither had bothered politicians for a long time, but then there were other things to do.

By the mid-1970s, the then Labour Prime Minister James Callaghan, initiated the great debate in his now famous speech at Ruskin College in October, 1976. It was a golden opportunity to answer the critics, to defend and advance the educational interest, but the Prime Minister, concerned at what he saw as the impact the Conservative party's criticisms were making on public opinion, chose to take the schools to task. The basis of his criticism was that the schools failed to provide what the nation needed — young people who had the relevant skills and attributes required by society.

The great debate in the late 1970s centred on a number of major, interrelated issues: the relevance of the school curriculum to the world of work; the supposed inadequacy of the standards attained by school leavers in the three Rs, their general level of knowledge, or lack of it, in other subject areas; the attitude of schools towards industry, said to be isolationist and unfriendly, and the involvement of parents in the educational decision making process, assumed to be non-existent; hence the establishment of the Taylor Committee, with terms of reference designed to remedy this situation and break the supposed stranglehold of the professional teachers over the schools.

Why did the great debate start at all? Why did politicians appoint themselves to 'sort out' the schools? Why was it that such a lot that had previously been right, was now wrong? There was certainly no revolution among parents, the vast majority of whom not only accepted readily the schools to which they sent their children, but supported what teachers achieved – as shown by the record growth of the numbers of pupils in voluntary attendance in secondary schools throughout the 1960s and 1970s. The extension of higher and further education, with more and more young people seeking access to universities, the spread of new polytechnics and further education colleges, the unique pioneering enterprise developed by the Open University, showed a demand for more education generated at school level. The great debate was certainly neither inspired nor wanted by those who were most intimately connected with the schools, the parents and the teachers. It was a political act based on the understandable concern of the then prime minister that the Conservatives might upstage Labour in the next election by successfully portraying the deficiencies of the school system.

The major instrument chosen to attack the schools' freedom was the curriculum. A Green Paper[10] recommended a review by local education authorities of curricular arrangements, and ominously stated that there would be consultation 'on the nature of any advice which will be issued to local education authorities on curriculum matters'. Thus, a decision to intervene centrally had already been taken. What then were the points at issue and how do they stand up to examinations in the real world of the schools where youngsters and teachers work togther, seeking to achieve harmony, rather than the constant controversy so beloved by politicians? First, there was the recommendation to 'protect' part of the curriculum to achieve aims 'common to all schools and pupils at certain stages, including the achievement of basic literacy and numeracy at the primary stage'. Spelling and arithmetic were named as the parts of the curriculum which needed protection. This is arrant nonsense. Literacy and numeracy are involved whatever children weigh, count, design, measure in any lessons or activity requiring these processes; to suggest that language and mathematical skills can be separated from other studies in school will be immediately recognisable by any teachers as artificial and unworkable. The Senior Inspector of the Department of Education and Science, Sheila Browne, who has shown a refreshing independence of thought throughout her term of office, in a speech to the conference of local education authorities in 1977, said that the primary school curriculum was 'pretty traditional, not subject to great variation in major respects, and gives priority to the basic skills — reading, writing and the spoken word and then to mathematics'. Certainly, prior to the great debate, the inspectorate saw no need for concern.

Next, there was the recommendation that 'schools must prepare for the transition to adult and working life: pupils are required to understand how the democratic system functions, the mixed economy, industrial activity and especially manufacturing which creates our national wealth'. The priority accorded to manufacturing is hardly a forward looking concept in the day of the computer and the silicon chip, and in an age when Britain is slowly, painfully, shedding its manufacturing image and turning into a technological society, just as it had to shed its image as an agricultural nation a century ago. Such political thinking lacks both perspective and vision. But even so, a main growth area in schools has been the development of school links with industry; works experience schemes had got off the ground in thousands of schools throughout the 1950s and 1960s, long before the Great Debate, sometimes in the face of difficulties or even hostility from authorities, employers, and at times, even from the trade unions. There was certainly no lack of interest, nor lack of willingness, on the part of the schools to work closely with industry.

However, the merit of the great debate was that it brought together teachers, inspectors, local education officers, employers, politicians and parents in the regional meetings initiated by the then Secretary of State, Shirley Williams. It was not to be expected that such a diversity of interests could at a few meetings, arrive at conclusions, and even less so, at consensus. But at least there was a desire on the part of the leading politicians to have a debate. Shirley Williams, and her Junior Ministers, Margaret Jackson and Gordon Oakes, stalked the country, chaired meetings, talked, and inevitably listened; the different parties present also listened to each other. This was not only a useful but genuine attempt at open government, which the teaching profession welcomed, and which, given the same orientation of some future government, is a development worth supporting. Firm views by politicians and others on the part that teachers should play in relating their professional work to the world outside schools can perfectly well exist alongside a readiness to discuss issues which highlight what help the schools can expect from politicians, employers and other consumer interests. During the great debate, the teachers took the opportunity to state their expectations, on behalf of the pupils, to the representatives of industry and commerce. Some employers learned for the first time what could be achieved by lively school-industry links. What was said was not always agreeable to one or the other party present, but it cleared the air and widened horizons all round.

The same cannot be said of more recent government policies on the curriculum. In November, 1979, the then Secretary of State, Mark Carlisle, stated his intention to 'establish broad agreement with the partners in the education service on a framework for the curriculum, and to examine whether parts of the curriculum should be protected because there are parts common to all schools and all pupils at certain stages'. Alongside this seemingly reasonable statement there was, however, a new approach, requesting local education authorities (but not the schools) to exercise 'leadership' and 'interpret national policies and objectives in the light of local needs'. In January, 1980, the government published a detailed document 'A Framework for the School Curriculum'.[11] The directions in which this moved were very clear: the government assigned to itself the 'inescapable duty to satisfy itself that the work of the schools matches national needs'. But nowhere are such national needs defined. What are they? Who agrees on them? In a democratic state, where political control is likely to change at elections, concepts of 'national needs' if defined at all, change also and it is absurd to ask schools to conform to curricular patterns reflecting such needs. Is there not a national need for young people to have jobs when they leave school, and to have training for such jobs?

Central recipes on the curriculum spell out in considerable detail what government expects to happen. A list of school aims is provided: pupils should be educated 'to develop lively minds, to apply themselves to tasks, to have religious and moral values'. In fact, standards are set which are not attained anywhere in the adult world. The suggested structure of the curriculum has a heavy emphasis on the 'common core'; the core curriculum itself is seen largely in subject terms — English, mathematics, science, modern languages, religious and physical education are the main pillars. The notion of growing points, the need to be alive to developments in electronics, environmental and communication studies, in computer work, which will need to be the ingredients of education for life in the next century, is unknown to the centralists; the concept of a dynamic curriculum, responsive to technological and social change is absent. The 'hidden curriculum', an understanding that this embraces the totality of all activities which go on in a school and contributes to the development and well-being of the individual, is inconceivable to the central planner. The culmination of the latest move towards centralism is Sir Keith Joseph's nominated Curriculum Council, to be set up in place of the Schools Council.[12] If persuasion will not work, the schools, and the teachers and children in them, will do as they are told.

This latest move means that the government is seeking to usurp responsibilities which properly belong to the schools, their teachers and their governing bodies in partnership with their parents, to do what each school considers best for its pupils, bearing in mind its staffing, building, general level of resource provision, type of intake, links with the local community, requirements of employers in the locality, expectations of parents, and many other variables. If the schools of the future are to have any chance at all to make effective contributions to improve the quality of life, to meet the challenge of living in the twenty-first century, they must not be encased in the kind of strait-jacket which today's politicians in power seek to impose. Diversity is an essential part of the human race and ought to be encouraged, not suppressed. There is no merit in standardising everything for everybody, except that it looks neat on paper to those who like that sort of neatness. The teaching profession of the 1980s needs to rouse itself to resist to the utmost the imposition of codes reminiscent of the reign of Napoleon and say clearly and unequivocally, that we must do our own job in our own way, without harassment, and without the intrusion on the teachers day-to-day work with the children.

The desire of the politicians to dominate educational thought and practice contrasts sharply with the attitudes of those concerned most intimately with schools — teachers, pupils and parents. Teachers, when confronted with policies and pronouncements by people whose knowledge of and acquaintance with present schools is, at best, years out of date and at worst, non-existent — are at first bewildered and subsequently resentful, at what is more and more clearly emerging as double talk; a promise, on the one hand, to the electorate to provide better opportunities, and press for higher standards however ill-defined, whilst at the same time reducing the resources needed to do a decent job in the classroom. Such resentment soon forms itself into opposition, not always, and not necessarily, against a particular political party, but against the whole concept of the political control of schools, for this is what a centralised curriculum inevitably brings. The direction which educational affairs will take in the 1980s depends largely on the determination of teachers, not only to resist the politicians, but to take a powerful hand themselves in educational reform – a real challenge to the profession.

The pupils themselves, whilst displaying healthy concern with what they do, rather than with what older generations talk about, see all too clearly what is happening, once they have reached sufficient maturity to appreciate the issues. In the fifth and sixth forms of our secondary schools, whether public or private, there is emerging a new attitude towards politics which must be taken seriously; it is a growing feeling among the young that the political system is incapable of solving the major problems of our day; whether they are growing unemployment, and increasing social conflict at home, or the great issues of world hunger and world peace involving the very survival of the human race. The young often see the world of adults as one gone mad in its obsession to argue, to score debating points, to exercise power. The teenager of the 1960s frequently supported one or the other of the two main political parties; the youngster of the 1980s tends to turn his back on the party political process as such, and one reason for this is certainly the realisation that the schools, the natural and accepted meeting places of young people of all beliefs, social background and frequently, different ethnic groups, do not enjoy the support, but attract the censure, and even hostility of those who govern. The young see this as an attack on themselves, because they think of the schools as their schools.

The attitude of parents differs little from those of either teachers or pupils. Where parental opinion finds organised expression, either at school or at national level, there is strong and consistent opposition to cuts in educational expenditure, and the philosophies associated with it. The major parent-orientated national body, the National Federation of Parent/Teacher Associations – is in the foreground of opposition to the cuts, and to the philosophy of central control of the curriculum. At school level, there is not a single parent/teacher association anywhere in the country on record in favour of accepting the present policy of retrenchment in education. But parental attitudes are not only concerned with maintaining the material fabric of the education service; parents want less controversy about schools, less uncertainty about what is to happen tomorrow, more security for their children, and above all, the strong desire that schools near their home, known to so many of them, will continue to exist, hence the opposition to the many school closures, leading to more upheaval and more mess and in the eyes of parents, creating areas of educational desert, both in cities and in villages.

This great gap between the aspirations of those who are the recipients of the educational process, and those who are the providers, shows every sign of widening. This is a serious matter not only for education as such, but for the quality of democratic life within our society. The teachers need to understand how and where this divergence has arisen and must be determined to narrow this gap, both for the sake of the nation's children and for the profession. The political process in the 1980s works against, rather than for, education. The pressure to provide resources for an ageing population, for the socially deprived, makes the social services, rather than education, the growing point for public expenditure. The great need is for the educational fraternity to demonstrate that the great social problems of today and tomorrow can only be coped with satisfactorily by improving the quality of education; compassion for the old, the sick and the deprived is an attitude of mind which the schools need, and indeed, do, seek to foster. Compassion finds its expression in action; thousands of schools set an example to their elders by their involvement in local service projects; frequent visits to old peoples' homes, to talk to the old, to tend their gardens, and inviting them to the school. Hundreds of projects for the physically and mentally handicapped find a place in school activities, in spite of the pressures of an examination ridden and subject dominated curriculum; such efforts do not make headlines, and cannot be expressed in percentage passes of 'O' and 'A' level, but they provide the essential human dimension of the educational process. Moves to centralise the curriculum, the pressure for the publication of examination results, emphasising the competitive aspects of school life, cuts in school budgets, and, the greatest evil of all, making thousands of teachers redundant, are therefore attacks not only on the teachers, but on the schools and the children. In essence, the schools are part of the fabric of civilised life, functioning on the basis of understanding human needs, and seek to meet these by enlightened, progressive curricula, responsive to local needs.

How should teachers react in such a situation? What can they do not only to protect their own jobs, but the interests of the children for whom they are responsible? How can they come to terms with a professional conscience which frequently prevents many teachers from striking, or indeed, from taking any militant action at all, for whatever action taken must affect their pupils unfavourably, at least in the short run. Chapter three examines how far the teachers' unions are likely to resist successfully further political interventionism; but the need is for every teacher to help change a climate which enables politicians in power to downgrade the education service.

It is essential for teachers to understand, to communicate to parents in particular, and to the general public at large, the difference between the educational and the political process. The political process is one which esentially thrives on controversy, and healthy controversy is the lifeblood of a democracy. The educational process on the other hand, essentially requires harmony and the establishment of harmonious relationships between pupils, teachers and parents, in an institutional framework − the school. The attack on teaching, being political, therefore requires, regrettably, a counter attack, the basis of which must be to challenge the politicians' view that their position gives them the right to say how our schools should be run. This must not, of course, be confused with attacking the democratic process as such; indeed, many politicians are worthy individuals, work hard and conduct their affairs for what they conceive to be the good of society. However, their besetting sin is to bring the essential ingredients of party politics onto the educational scene; the place for fighting for power or retaining it, once it has been gained, is the arena of the political parties and not the governing bodies of schools; the opportunities for powerful advocacy of particular economic and political policies lie in the council chambers locally and in the Houses of Parliament nationally, and not at the meetings of parent/teacher associations. Decisions on resource allocations lie inevitably, and rightly, with the elected representatives of the people, though their responsibility should not extend to detailed prescriptions as to how schools should spend their money. In a school, every decision, whether it relates to the allocation of resources, or the organisation of the curriculum, must be governed by adherence to the principle that schools exist for the good of the individual pupil, who is part of a school community which should give maximum benefit and happiness to those who constitute it. The application of principles of cost effectiveness, of highly competitive mechanisms, imply the tearing apart of institutions whose lives are based on different criteria from those which operate either in industry or in politics. The presumption that politicians are there to decide all questions relating to education, whether it is resource allocation, school systems, the curriculum or parent/teacher relations, needs to be challenged and the people to challenge it are the teachers, for there is no one else.

There is, in logic, no justification for an extension of political power into schools; those who enter politics, here, or indeed, elsewhere in the world, have not been markedly successful in dealing with the great global problems of world hunger, preventing people from killing each other in wars, or in promoting economic stability and social harmony. There is no inalienable right given to politicians, no principles of democratic government, which support the notion that the educational process requires either political intervention, or a high degree of political control. The universities, which are, after all, educational institutions, function without either; it is the Universities Grants Committee, a professional body, which deals with the details of resource allocation once global sums have been settled. There has been no discernible movement among the political parties, no prime minister's advocacy of the content of degree courses. The essential need for independence at the top of the educational pyramid is acknowledged. Why should it not apply to schools? The principle of non-intervention is respected in the other great professions — doctors, lawyers and the clergy are not subjected to detailed reviews of the content of their practices, or to monitoring or testing of the services they provide. Why should school teachers be treated differently? Once teachers have been trained and appointed, once schools have been established and a system of accountability worked out, they must be allowed to get on with the job. This is not to say that there should be no changes in the method of doing things; schools reflect society and since society itself is changing, schools must inevitably change and be dynamic and forward looking institutions. But they cannot and should not be seen as the party political battleground which they have become in the last couple of decades, and are likely to remain if the politicians of the 1980s have their way. What is needed to be 'de-politicisation' of the work of the schools, a deliberate removal of educational issues from being used as causes to gain votes, to enhance progress in politics, to enable those with no real connection with the schools to parade as spokesman for, or often against, education. The true professional teacher, who cares about the welfare and happiness of the pupils under his care, and feels keenly his responsibility towards the parent who entrust him with their children, can only fulfil his task if he is free from doctrinaire, political interventionists and prepared to stand up for the interests of education whenever and wherever it is under attack.

Notes

1. DES Annual Report for 1981 (HMSO, London, 1982) reveals that 217 closures were approved by the Secretary of State of which 183 were primary schools.

2. See 'Report by Her Majesty's Inspectors on the Effects of Local Authority Expenditure Policies on the Education Service in England, 1981' (HMSO, London, March, 1982).

3. See report of Expenditure Steering Group for Education, reported in *Times Educational Supplement*, 9 July 1982, p. 1.

4. In Spring 1982, the Barking Authority attempted to sack 90 teachers, but withdrew the sackings after a ten week teachers' strike organised by the NUT.

5. See Chapter six which examines the activities of the APU.

6. See Chapter five.

7. One of the most blatant attempts by extreme Conservative party politicians to demolish a good comprehensive school, the Erith School in Kent, failed. The school was formed some ten years ago by the amalgamation of two neighbouring schools, and had achieved a respectable academic record, coupled with an extremely good reputation for its involvement in local community projects. The Kent County Council, after the general election in 1979, decided to re-establish selective education in the area. The Director of Education was instructed to prepare plans to divide the school, making one part of it a selective grammar, and the other a secondary modern school. The local politicians did not wait until the necessary consent was obtained from the Secretary of State, feeling confident that the new Conservative administration would support its plans.

The writer was involved in meetings with teachers in the Erith School and in deputations to Baroness Young, then Minister of Education, to stop the scheme. It was evident that the effect on the morale of the teaching staff, pupils and parents, was disastrous. The proposed destruction of a well-established school, caused a public outcry in Erith; it was clear that the proposal had no popular support. The new Conservative Secretary of State was faced with a difficult decision; was he to follow the party line as seen by the most extreme members of the party, or should he judge the case on its merits? It is to Mark Carlisle's credit that, when the scheme was finally referred to him for approval, he rejected it, and thus maintained the present Erith school.

8. 'Foundation for the Future – an Education and Training Policy' – SDP green paper, No. 4, London, July, 1982.

9. See Dr Boyson's speech to Dover and Deal Conservatives, reported in *Times Educational Supplement*, 30 July 1982 and *The Times* 24 July 1982. Dr Boyson advocated vouchers cashable both at state and independent schools, and the operation of a 'market economy' in education.

10. 'Education in Schools – a Consultative Document', Cmnd 6869 (HMSO, London, July, 1977).

11. 'A Framework for the School Curriculum' (HMSO, London, January, 1980).

12. See Chapter three for an examination of the Trenaman review of the Schools Council and Sir Keith Joseph's proposals.

2 THE POLITICAL SCENE: THE BATTLE FOR RESOURCES

The educational system operates in a political context; all major decions are made by politicians, either nationally or locally, and are part of the complicated relationship between local and central government. The overriding power of the elected members of parliament and local councillors to decide the allocation of resources, the structure of the school system, the procedures relating to the appointment and promotion of teachers, their pay and conditions of service, has never been seriously challenged, and is seen as part of the responsibility of government for the education services laid down in successive Education Acts. The Secretary of State for Education and Science is a member of the Cabinet, and, as the political head of the Department of Education and Science, is accountable to Parliament for all aspects of state education. Since the establishment of compulsory education in 1870, the administration of education has been seen as a partnership between local authorities and central government, and although the balance of power between the two has varied according to circumstances, issues, personalities of Minister, there has been, among all political parties, among the public, and in the teaching profession, a consensus that this partnership implies a locally administered service, with resources provided jointly by central and local government. The real essence of political control therefore lies in the allocation of resources to education, and the political decisions which determine the level of resources, determine everything else — the number of teachers employed, policies relating to the opening and closing of schools, the shape of the school system, the capitation allowances available to individual schools for the purchase of books and equipment, the state of the buildings, the provision of grants for students, for transport, for in-service training, and the staffing standards within schools and education offices.

During the last five years, two fundamental changes have occurred in the relationship between central and local government, which have vitally affected the provision of resources for education: the first relates to the declining share of the cost of local services borne by central government, and the second is the greater control exercised by the centre over the expenditure of local authorities. The following table

19

Table 2.1: Financing of Local Government Expenditure in England

Financial Year	The Government's Contribution	The Local Authorities Contribution
1980–1	61%	39%
1981–2	59%	41%
1982–3	56%	44%

Source: NUT Document 'Education: The Fight for our Childrens' Future' – January, 1982.

shows how the government has shifted an increasing share of the cost of local services from money gained through taxes to the local rate-payers.

These cuts have been effected through the Rate Support Grant mechanism (RSG), the lump sum allocated by government to local authorities for expenditure on all services: the education service is financed through sums allocated to the Department of Education and Science and these too, have been subjected to progressive cuts. The declining share available for the education service is part of a process which became significant in the early 1970s; between 1973 and 1976, cuts of nearly £1,500 million were announced by government; and whilst cuts were less severe between 1976 and 1979, the position has worsened considerably since 1979 and is likely to get even worse. The declining share of the education service as such, compared with services for defence, health, law and order, and social security, emerges clearly from the figures published by the government itself.

Table 2.2: Spending on Selected Functions as a Percentage of Total UK Public Expenditure, 1978/9–1983/4

	1978/9	1980/1	1983/4
Education and Science	12.7	12.1	11.6
Defence	11.6	12.3	13.6
Health	14.3	14.2	15.5
Law and Order	4.0	4.2	4.6
Social Security	24.6	25.7	29.1
Overseas Aid	2.6	2.1	2.0
Total (includes functions not listed above)	100	100	100

Source: Cmnd. 8175, HMSO, London.

In percentage terms, the period 1978–84, according to government plans, will see a reduction in spending on education to 11.6 per cent, as against increases in defence, in health, in law and order and in social security. The reasons given by government are that the reduced allocation is all the country can afford, and that falling rolls in schools allow reductions to be made which, it has been argued, will not affect educational standards. However, the period 1978–84 will see a fall in rolls by only 8.8 per cent, against projected cuts to 11 per cent. There is no doubt that the ruling politicians accord education a lower priority than other services.

The second change has been in the manner in which central government has resorted to increasingly rigid and restrictive measures to limit local authorities in the exercise of their judgment to determine their own priorities for the services they administer. This is done in two ways. First, there are the cash limits, limits which the government puts on public spending programmes, beyond which there are no extra allowances to compensate for inflation, or salary settlements beyond certain limits. Thus, if the teachers succeed in getting a salary increase of 6 per cent and the government provides for only 4 per cent, the difference must be found either by raising the rates, or reducing the numbers of teachers employed; the cash limit system, which started in 1976 thus has an in-built cutback of its own. Second, legislation, still proceeding through parliament in the shape of the Local Government Finance Bill,[1] limits any increases in rates which local authorities may wish to make, with power to fix the rate, in certain circumstances, being exercised by the Secretary of State for the Environment himself, assisted by a new organisation, an Audit Commission for local authorities, which will also undertake studies of the efficiency of local services. The policy is to remove, step by step, the freedom of local authorities to determine their policies and priorities; it is essentially a change in the philosophy of the political process, a style of government based firmly on the notion that it is central government, through its ministers and its civil service, that makes the big decisions, and no longer the local authorities. The whole trend of policies, since the Conservative Government took office in 1979, is in the direction of centralism, although there were signs of such developments throughout the 1970s. In essence, therefore, the attack on teaching identified in Chapter one is also an attack on local government, and, in its more extreme manifestations, an attack on local democracy itself. The notion that local councillors and officials are less fitted than the ministers, and civil servants operating control systems designed centrally is firmly entrenched in Westminster. The belief that the education ministers and officials at Elizabeth House, the headquarters of the Department of Education and Science, are 'in charge of schools and teachers', and know better than those who actually work in the schools every day, what is best for the nation's children, is fundamental to the philosophy of today's government. What is happening in the political arena are not only reductions in the amounts of money for education, nor changes in the manner in which this is distributed; there is a belief, emerging clearly from legislation, parliamentary replies and public speeches, that 'strong' government at the centre is not only necessary to save the nation, but that the saviours rule by a kind of divine right.

But the total level of resource provision by central government can only tell part of the story; what concerns every pupil, every parent,

Table 2.3: Local Education Authority Spending, 1980–1

London	Pupil Teacher Ratio		Spending per child on books and equipment (gross)		Total unit costs (net)	
	Primary	Secondary	Prim £	Sec £	Prim £	Sec £
ILEA	17.5	14.3	40	75	927	1,270
Metropolitan Districts						
Greater Manchester						
Bolton	24.3	16.2	16	29	491	741
Merseyside						
Liverpool	20.8	16.1	18	35	612	896
South Yorkshire						
Sheffield	21.2	16.3	23	28	614	818
West Midlands						
Birmingham	23.2	16.4	11	27	530	777
Dudley	24.1	17.4	14	26	471	688
English Counties						
Buckinghamshire	23.9	16.7	17	32	526	821
Essex	24.4	17.7	14	24	496	757
Isles of Scilly	13.9	11.5	12	27	812	1,435
Norfolk	22.2	17.2	14.	26	536	773
Northamptonshire	24.0	17.3	13	28	496	734
Somerset	24.7	18.3	13	25	492	723
Welsh Counties						
Clwyd	22.9	17.0	15	25	547	758
Powys	18.7	15.9	12	24	707	899
National Aggregates						
London (21)	20.2	15.2	25	48	726	1,011
Met districts (36)	22.4	16.4	15	26	559	765
Non-Met districts (47)	23.1	17.0	15	26	529	765
All authorities	22.6	16.6	16	29	560	795

Source: *Times Educational Supplement*, 9 July 1982, p. 6. (Number of local authorities in brackets.) Statistics provided by CIPFA (Chartered Institute of Public Finance and Accounting).

every teacher, is what happens in his locality, and indeed, in his school. Here, the wide disparities which show just how much money the 104 local education authorities in England and Wales actually spend must be the cause of major concern. Table 2.3 shows a sample of local authorities comparing the highest, the lowest, and average spenders, as well as showing an aggregate picture.

Congratulations are due to the Isles of Scilly as the most generous provider for its 308 pupils, and to the Inner London Education Authority, which manages to lead the field with a £927 spending on each primary and £1,270 on each secondary pupil! No doubt, a hundred and four different reasons could be advanced by all 104 local education authorities to explain the variations; however, the conclusion that the biggest, the most telling factor is the political will in the local areas is inescapable. Whatever problems in the localities, whatever the strains and stresses caused by the demands of different services, whatever the shape and size of the bargain between an individual local authority and the government, the total pattern showing figures for every authority must, and does, indicate, the degree of priority given to education in each area. Wherever and whenever local politicians assume the right to make judgments on the quality of teaching in the schools — and no one denies them this right — so it is surely not only the right, but the duty of every teacher to relate such judgments to the resources provided. Every teacher knows that the quality of the teaching process is vitally affected by the number of teachers per number of children, the availability, or absence, of teaching support time, the size of classes, the provision of books, materials and equipment, the quality of the school environment, and the many other influences which bear upon classroom situations. It is a message which cannot be spelt out too often, and too urgently, by the teachers. Not that the teachers are without allies in spelling it out. The disparity between resources available in different areas has long been a matter of concern, and the most recent ideas[3] from the government itself gives some recognition to the need to finance education, at least, in part, by returning to the education block grant, with some 75 per cent of educational expenditure being found by the government, and the remainder by local authorities.

The return to the block grant has political implications, and is part of the struggle for control between local and central government; it is not surprising, therefore, that views differ sharply on the issue, differences which emerged forcefully at the 1982 summer meeting[4] of the Society of Education Officers, the body to which the vast majority of senior education officers of local authorities belong. Opinions among the education officers were divided and no clear cut policy emerged; the guest speaker, Professor John Stewart, of the Institute of Local Government Studies in Birmingham, argued that block grants would inevitably mean interference with local business by central government, and were more likely to control high spending authorities than to encourage lower spenders towards more effort; Christopher Price, MP, the distinguished and knowledgeable Chairman of the House of Commons Select Committee on Education, Sciences and the Arts, speaking at the same gathering, believed that 'power follows the pound' and thus joined the anti-block grant camp, although his assessment that, in the last analysis, it required some future Prime Minister to restore education's role by an 'important statement' is both shrewd and true; he clearly sees the need to reverse the judgmental stance started by James Callaghan's Ruskin Speech, at the highest level. But some anti-block grant arguments surely beg the question! Is there not already sufficient evidence that central government does interfere with local authorities? Every education officer, every education committee member in every part of the country is continually conscious, and their deliberations overshadowed, by what central government will allow or not allow, and pay for and not pay for. The teachers have little to lose, and much to gain, by a return to a specific block grant for education, and it is not surprising that both the National Union of Teachers, and the Secondary Heads Association support it. SHA,[5] in particular, urges that the size of the block grant should be determined by the Department of Education and Science, and not by any other government department, and also recommends additional specific grants for particular purposes.

The headteacher members of both the NUT and SHA have day-to-day responsibility for the distribution of their capitation allowances within their schools and know what they are talking about. Whilst individual school budgets vary as much as patterns of expenditure between different local education authorities, there can be no doubt that every school, every teacher and every child has been adversely, and often very seriously, affected by the cuts.

However, it is one thing for teachers to point out the paucity of provision for the nation's children, but quite another to have the argument accepted, or even seriously examined. Teachers who sit as co-opted members on education committees up and down the country are often accused by elected councillors of 'crying wolf'; of painting a picture of underprovision when the reality shows that schools are managing 'quite well', of simply protecting their own interests. Who is to make judgments on the quality of schooling, and inevitably on the quality of teaching? Whose word is to be taken, and trusted, in making judgments on the relationship between resource allocation and the quality of the service? It is important, therefore, to turn for evidence on the effects of the political process to the findings of impartial observers, Her Majesty's Inspectorate. HMIs are politically independent; they do not have day-to-day responsibility to the Secretary of State, but inspect schools according to their own criteria and professional judgments. They report as they see the situation in the country's schools during their visits.

In February, 1981, the Department of Education and Science took the unprecedented step of publishing a report by the HMIs[6] on the effects of the reduction in expenditure in the schools; a year later in March, 1982[7] there was a further report, and both tell the same sorry story: the first report surveyed 900 school premises in England and found 300 to be in a poor state, owing to reductions in programmes for maintenance, repairs and redecoration. In nearly four fifths of local authorities, the amount of money available for books, materials and equipment had been reduced compared with the previous year. Outworn and outdated books were becoming commonplace, and the HMIs commented that often teachers had to restort to demonstrations in science and other lessons, rather than letting the pupils conduct experiments, owing to lack of funds for equipment. It is relevant here to note that the Director of the Educational Publishing Council claimed that four million fewer school books were purchased in 1980 than in 1979, and that in real terms, spending on books was about 60 per cent of the 1975 level. Cuts in non-teaching staff in all categories — classroom ancillaries, technicians, library staff, clerical staff and foreign language assistants occurred in nearly all authorities. The reduction in foreign language assistants was particulary disastrous, some 400 fewer being employed than in 1979.

The HMIs said that the amount and range of in-service training was satisfactory in only about half of the local authorities. There was a substantial trend away from courses involving the release of teachers in school time to part-time courses attended by teachers of their own time. The report stated:

There was evidence of reduced takeup of all kinds of in-service training as a result of the problems of reduced supply cover because of the greater difficulty teachers had in obtaining financial assistance when attending courses.[8]

Nine-tenths of local authorities actually reduced the number of teachers they employed between November, 1979 and November, 1980 and just over 10,000 full-time posts disappeared during that period, from a total teaching force of about 470,000. Whilst the majority of such posts were lost through 'natural wastage', i.e. teachers leaving and not being replaced, there was also evidence of severe curtailment in the appointment of part-time and supply teachers. The HMIs noted that local authorities appeared to have taken a great deal of trouble to avoid compulsory redundancies; no doubt the resistance put up by the teachers' unions had some effect. However, in many secondary schools the inspectors found evidence that teachers were teaching subjects for which they were inadequately qualified or not qualified at all; they found large teaching groups and classes of children widely mixed in ability or age or both. In the primary schools there was evidence of increasing pressure on headteachers to undertake heavy teaching responsibilities and having to make a choice between reasonably sized classes and no remedial teaching, or large classes, with a continuation of small remedial groups. The reduction in non-teaching staff meant that heads were frequently torn between administrative and teaching responsibilities. The NUT collected detailed information on the cuts in March, 1981 and again in July, 1982[9] listing both the areas and the subjects affected. Figures released in September, 1982 indicated that class sizes of well over 30 were becoming much more common, and that mixed-aged teaching was on the increase. The worst areas were said to be Barnsley, Trafford, Oxfordshire, Warwickshire, Manchester, Bexley and Croydon. Primary schools in Oxfordshire averaged 32 children per class.

The worsening shortage of basic equipment, particularly books, which is also highlighted in the report of the HMIs, was found to be particularly bad in Surrey where some pupils wrote on computer paper because exercise books were not available, and in Croydon, where some pupils had to pay a £10 deposit on GCE and CSE books before they were allowed to take them home for study. This clearly must have a serious effect on children from poorer families.

Supply teaching also showed cuts which were sometimes heavy. In Hereford and Worcester, supply cover is only available after six weeks absence, and in Manchester and Gwent, after two weeks. In Durham, it was stated there would be no supply cover at all in secondary schools. Such measures go hand in hand with cuts in staffing, but not always in line with the falling rolls. In Kingston-upon-Thames, for example, a 2 per cent reduction in pupils over the last three years was matched by an 8 per cent cut in the number of staff. Hertfordshire, in the coming year, is to scrap 419 teaching posts, whereas a reduction of 245 would maintain its existing pupil/teacher ratios. Similar worsening of ratios are likely to take place in Surrey (345 posts likely to be scrapped as against 245 to maintain pupil/teacher ratios) and Manchester (333 as against 200). Remedial teaching was severely cut in Gwent, Kent and Trafford, and there was reduced provision in Cambridgeshire, Hampshire, Norfolk, Leicestershire, Staffordshire, Surrey, Wiltshire, Barnsley, Bradford, Coventry, Newcastle and Solihull. Music took some punishment, with charges for instrument tuition being imposed in Bedfordshire, Buckinghamshire, Cornwall, Dorset, East Sussex, Essex, Oxfordshire, Somerset, Rochdale and Redbridge. In Hereford and Worcestershire, music tuition stopped altogether in some schools; other areas affected were home economics and foreign language teaching. Hampshire appointed no more Spanish foreign language assistants and Surrey dropped French in 25 per cent of its middle schools. Newcastle-upon-Tyne was reported as closing its immigrant language centre. Sport was also similarly affected. Kent cut back in specialist coaching and charges for swimming were imposed in Bedfordshire, Buckinghamshire and Solihull. Transport charges in Hereford and Worcestershire, Kent, Gateshead, Solihull and Stockport affected some swimming programmes. There were reports of seven pools being closed in Sefton and some in Solihull and Brent. Swimming provision was further reduced in Avon, Cornwall, Northumberland, Mid-Glamorgan, Bradford, Gateshead, Rochdale and Merton. The library service was also severely affected: out of 68 local education authorities with a school library service, only eleven allowed inflation proof budget increases in 1979/80. During that period there was an overall 8 per cent drop in spending.

A further report published a year later[10] allows some comparisons to be made with the position reported in the earlier one. It was based on a large number of visits made by individual HMIs to schools, and on an analysis of 2,126 returns, covering expenditure patterns and effects on the curriculum in 1,761 schools. The HMIs said specifically that they were reporting on the standard of available educational provision, and assessing its effect on the quality of work observed. 'They are judging whether what they observe is good enough, not whether levels of provision and quality of education have changed since last year as a result of financial policies.' One could ask for no greater impartiality.

The returns studied by the HMIs covered teaching staff, non-teaching staff, in-service training, induction, the advisory service, school premises, capitation allowances for books, materials and equipment.

With absolute fairness the HMIs stated that out of 71 LEAs which showed a reduction in allowances, the overall reductions could be described as slight in 55 areas, and moderate to considerable in the other 16. The 16 contained four LEAs whose level of provision gave real cause for concern. Eleven LEAs were said to have made better provision. The LEAs were not named.

On teaching staffs, the HMIs noted that the number of teachers in English schools contracted by more than 10,000 between September, 1980 and September, 1981, whilst at the same time the number of pupils fell by nearly 200,000. Again, the reduction was achieved mainly by natural wastage and early retirements. The pupil/teacher ratios had not shown a substantial change, but where changes had occurred they had more often been unfavourable, more so in the cases of secondary than primary schools. Of 23 local education authorities where the change in pupil/teacher ratio has been greater than .5, 13 worsened them within the range of .6 to 1.3. Ten local authorities however, improved their primary pupil/teacher ratio. Eight local authorities had worsened their overall secondary pupil/teacher ratio within a range of .6 to 1, and two had improved it.

The district inspectors reported that whilst the level of staffing in primary schools had not caused drastic overall change, in internal organisation there had been an increase in the number of mixed-aged classes in nearly a third of the local education authorities and also a reduction in the number of small teaching groups for remedial work. Observations were recorded in some 970 primary schools, of which 790 were judged to be satisfactory, the same proportion as last year. However, in the remaining schools, and particularly in small schools, the HMIs found evidence of loss of staff through falling rolls and the stricter application of staffing formula, which worsened pupil/teacher ratios, and sometimes led to inflexibility in organisation. 'This makes it difficult at best, impossible at worst, to provide remedial teaching or to respond to pupils with a range of special learning needs, or to provide specialist help for parts of the curriculum requiring particular subject knowledge.'[11]

In the secondary schools the HMIs reported changes in the curriculum in the form of reduction in the range of courses offered. This applied to one-third of the authorities, especially those in the shire counties. Examples quoted included the elimination of such courses as child care and motor vehicle technology, in the fourth and fifth years, less provision for remedial work, physical education, instrumental music, and sixth form general studies. Again, the inspectors found an increasing incidence of subjects being taught by teachers who did not hold appropriate specialist qualifications. In small secondary schools in eleven local education authorities, inadequate staffing levels and range of qualifications were judged to be having a bad effect.

A total of 932 individual HMIs visited secondary schools and sixth form colleges and found that about a fifth of these suffered from too few appropriately qualified staff. Examples related to virtually all areas of the curriculum, but most frequently referred to craft, design and technology, history, art and design and courses for the least able pupils. Again, there were reports of teachers being asked to teach subjects which were not their main specialism in most areas of the curriculum, and included English, mathematics, modern languages and science; a few reports spoke of subjects disappearing altogether from the curriculum; these included craft, design and technology and languages, with the elimination of a second modern language mentioned in four reports.

In the sphere of non-teaching staff, the HMIs stated that there was a continuing contraction of all categories of non-teaching staff. Although 13 LEAs had made small increases in individual categories, the provision of classroom ancillaries had decreased in 44; of librarians in 17, of technical assistants in 31, of clerical assistants in 48, and of language assistants in 16 LEAs. Other ancillary staff, particularly cleaners and gardeners, had been cut in 20 authorities. Overall the HMIs stated that the provision of non-teaching staff was entirely satisfactory in only 37 local authorities, compared with the two-thirds judged tolerable or better in the previous year.

Looking at capitation allowances, HMIs found that 19 authorities had increased them in real terms, whereas another 36 had reduced them, the remainder maintaining previous levels. However, the HMIs detected that 14 authorities had increased the range of items for which schools had to pay, which were previously funded separately; these included postage, telephone charges, cleaning materials and visits, field studies, furniture and repairs, and the maintenance of library book stocks. As far as library textbooks stock was concerned, the inspectors found that the position was satisfactory, or better, in just under half of the local authorities, compared with just over half last year. They commented on the fact that the London Boroughs as a group provided pupils significantly better with books than either the Metropolitan Districts or the Shire counties. Concern was expressed by 26 HMIs about the level of provision in school libraries. Less than satisfactory provision was indicated by 240 primary school returns, with acute shortages being referred in 15 instances. A total of 300 secondary schools reported a less than satisfactory provision, with acute shortages being mentioned in 33 returns.

With regard to materials and equipment, the report suggested some deterioration since the last time, with one-fifth of primary schools referring to individual shortages of equipment, including basic equipment and nearly one-quarter of returns from secondary schools and sixth form colleges noting a specific shortage, particularly in science, craft, design and technology and art.

Looking at school buildings, the HMIs recorded that maintenance and decoration were satisfactory in about three-quarters of primary and two-thirds of secondary schools, but comments mention 'educationally unsuitable environment provided by shabby and inadequately maintained buildings'. They also speak of occasional examples of 'rotting external joinery and leaking flat roofs'. The reports comment on funds raised by parents being used to improve the quality of the school premises, and state categorically that overall 'the stock on school premises is continuing to deteriorate and failure to maintain the fabric of some buildings has already presented at least two LEAs with heavy repair and renovation costs'.[12]

A significant feature of the HMIs report relates to parental contributions and other sources of funding: 'in virtually all LEAs parents are contributing to schools in cash, kind or labour to an increasing extent'. The inspectors found that in rather more than half of the local authorities, parents contributed to a moderate or considerable extent to the purchase of such basic items as books and materials. A year earlier, the HMIs had commented on the fact that some large schools were seeking the services of fund raising agencies and teaching staffs were devoting time to organising fund raising activities. HMIs commented particularly on fund raising activities, especially in the shire counties, and noted instances of parents contributing regular weekly, termly or annual payments. Examples include charges of £12.50 per head per annum in small rural schools, the raising of £9,000 in a large London primary school, £15,000 in a metropolitan grammar school, and £1,000 per annum in a shire primary school of 121 pupils. The report notes that this money is spent in various ways, including the purchase of books, acquisition of special instruments such as microscopes, sewing machines, welding equipment and musical instruments. HMIs note that whilst parents in the more affluent areas appear able and willing to respond to requests from schools, some 40 of the HMIs report refer to schools in areas of deprivation where headteachers feel unable to approach parents, and where fund raising events produce smaller sums.

With regard to the payment of examination fees, the report notes that the examination policies in about half the local education authorities impose some restriction on entries for which fees are paid by the authority. This applies to the re-sitting of exams, late entry fees, CSE 'conversions' to GCEs and double entries. There were also some limitations on the entries per candidate.

The general picture is not an encouraging one. HMIs, whilst commenting that the majority of pupils are still adequately served, state that:

> The awareness of schools and LEAs of the limitations set to what they can offer, generally evokes a determination to do everything possible, but is also professionally undermining. So too is the uncertainty caused by protracted discussion of reorganisations and closures.

With regard to primary schools, it is stated that further restraints on spending and falling rolls have continued to affect primary schools in the same way as last year. Increasingly, when teachers leave they are either not replaced, or replaced by teachers on short-term contracts, or redeployed teachers who may not fit the school's needs as far as curricular cover or age and ability range of pupils are concerned. There is a further comment about the deflection of headteachers from their proper role as setters of standards and leading curricular and educational reform. In the secondary schools, the report states that the financial restraints mentioned in the previous report were now beginning seriously to affect many secondary schools and adding to the unfavourable effects of restraints in spending over the past few years. The HMIs note the 'widening difference in provision across the country for pupils who have similar needs and abilities'.

Finally, the judgment of HMIs on the teachers themselves are worth quoting: the HMIs gained the impression of continued professional commitment and resourcefulness, but the teachers' morale was very thin as the uncertainties of changes arising from falling rolls and cuts in expenditure affected both the maintenance of present standards and attempts to bring about improvements.

Like other mortals, HMIs vary in perception, competence and powers of judgment; however, they have no axe to grind when they look at schools; they do not have to please anybody — teachers, local authorities' officers, or party politicians — when they go into schools. They may not see everything, and sometimes may miss what teachers feel they should see, or may be seen to attach importance to issues seen as trivial by class teachers. This is as it may be. What is beyond doubt are the findings of HMIs on the state of resources in the schools, following the wave of cuts in the last five years. If ever the teachers' case against the cuts needed vindication, here it is: the result of the political process, of political decision making on the day-to-day life of the schools, has been disastrous.

What can be done to improve the situation or to prevent, at the very least, arrest, a rapidly deteriorating level of resource provision in the 1980s? The pressures to reduce this provision in the light of falling school rolls, and competing demands within the public sector to meet other important needs, certainly for the social services, will continue to increase. There are no simple answers, but it is evident that politicians, by the very nature of their positions, are responsive to pressures as such. The education service, whilst under attack, and whilst having taken a great deal of punishment, provides itself examples of success stories: the level of expenditure maintained by the Inner London Education Authority in the face of enormous hostility from central government, including its threatened abolition; the reinstatement of the sacked headmistress Eileen Crosby in Nottinghamshire;[13] the successful NUT action to prevent teachers being sacked in Barking,[14] and the many battles fought in villages and cities to preserve schools scheduled for closure show that determination to resist the cuts, the mobilisation of public opinion in favour of education, the organisation of interest groups, particularly parents, to support educational objectives are by no means lost causes every time. What is needed is to ensure that such strong local initiatives have sufficient national cohesion to make an impact on the political process itself. To give it such cohesion is surely one of the major functions of the teachers' unions, to be described in the following chapter. But the task cannot be left to the unions, even if, on many issues, they are successful in preventing the worst from happening. What is needed is a realisation that on the major issues of resource provision, the interests of the teachers and the interests of the children are identical. The teachers must be seen to fight, not only for themselves, but for the children they teach. Every teacher, newly qualified, or well established, must help in the task of shaping public opinion in favour of the cause of education, and against the cuts. Such a stance need not, and should not be a party political one; teachers should of course, be perfectly free to engage in party politics in the same way as every other citizen, but in their professional role, they should fight the good fight for education against whichever party happens to be in power, if it seeks to impose cuts, or if it moves towards the centralist role which spells such damages to the service. There is every sign that initiatives by individual teachers and individual schools, often count for more than the verbal fire-eating which sometimes emerges from union conferences in response to similar stances taken up by politicians. Every school, each teacher, creates a reputation which influences and shapes the opinions of those immediately concerned with the school — parents, local employers, local politicians, a point which will be pursued in the final chapter — 'The Essence of Professionalism'. Here, it is relevant to note that the credibility of political parties with the electorate cannot be taken for granted, and there are signs that many members of the public do not think that party political motives are always the worthiest motives. Such a loss of credibility does not apply to anything like the same extent to teachers. The teacher's strength is his professionalism, not his party political views, which are no more, and no less, acceptable than anybody else's views. For this reason, the preservation of neutrality from party politics by the teachers' unions is essential. Parents need to feel that the teachers care for their children, because they feel a sense of professional responsibility, not because they support, or do not support, a particular political party.

It is also important to spell out a formula for financing education which takes the individual school as its starting point for budget calculations, rather than a place which receives its share at the end of a long drawn out process. How much does it cost to run a school? What textbooks, materials, equipment are needed to give reasonable lessons? How much should be set aside each year to preserve the fabric of the building and carry out essential repairs? What provisions must be made to preserve the essential curriculum even when rolls are falling and there is a risk that subjects may disappear from the timetable? The compilation and costing of a list of essential items to run a school is certainly well within the grasp of most heads and education officers. There is a deperate need to focus on the needs of individual schools and individual children, and remind the policy makers that this is what policy is all about — the welfare, happiness and progress of today's children and tomorrow's adults, which matters to them, their parents and their teachers. If the political process is to be at all meaningful in the next decade, there must emerge more politicians with the courage and vision to state their faith in the schools, and to preach the gospel that the education industry is an investment, and not a liability. Without teaching, which begins in the schools, there can be no accountants, no industrialists, and indeed, no politicians — they have all learned to read, write and count, because somewhere, at some time, a teacher has taught them. The purpose of the political process, as it affects education, is therefore, not the creation of controversy, but the promotion of harmony, which every child needs both at home and at school.

Notes

1. See text of Local Government Finance Bill — (No. 2) 1981 'Explanatory and Financial Memorandum' — the first bill was withdrawn after strong opposition to the idea of compelling local councils to hold referenda if they wished to resist cuts beyond the level set by the Secretary of State for the Environment.

2. The published table lists all local authorities.

3. Sir Keith Joseph, Education Secretary, is said to favour a return to the block grant.

4. See Report of Meeting of Society of Education Officers, *Times Educational Supplement,* 9 July 1982, p. 8.

5. The Secondary Headteachers' Association (SHA) reflects a widely-held view among school heads that a block grant would favour schools' allowances, whatever the economic restraints.

6. 'Report of Her Majesty's Inspectors on Effects of Local Authority Expenditure Policies on the Education Service in England', DES publication (HMSO, London, February, 1982).

7. Ibid., but published March, 1982.

8. Ibid.

9. See NUT circulars to local associations, Hamilton House, London (March, 1981; July, 1982 and September 1982).

10. 'Report of Her Majesty's Inspectors on Effects of Local Authority Expenditure Policies on the Education Services in England' (HMSO, London, March, 1982).

11. Ibid., p. 3.

12. Ibid., p. 8.

13. Eileen Crosby, headmistress of a Nursery School, was sacked by the Nottinghamshire County Council in 1979 for refusing to teach oversized classes, but was reinstated when the Labour party gained control of the council two years later.

14. After a teachers' strike in the Spring of 1982, the Labour controlled Barking Authority withdrew plans for the sackings.

3 THE TEACHERS' UNIONS

The teaching profession in the 1980s is faced with enormous challenges: first and foremost, there is the need to protect the interests of the children at a time when educational cuts are biting, the battle for resources is accelerating, and teacher redundancies are gathering momentum. Next, there is the struggle against the encroachment on the daily work of the schools, the determination of powerful politicians to centralise the curriculum and force upon the schools a pattern of learning values no longer acceptable to large numbers of students, teachers and parents: success in a competitive rat race reflected in examination marks and taking account of little else, an obsession with monitoring standards[1] which ignores changing values in society; finally, there is the need to resist the attack on the freedom of the teacher to do his own job in his own way, the very essence of professionalism. How can teachers resist such attacks? How can they influence educational affairs, the climate in which educational debates are conducted, and make an impact on the popular and political will which, in the final analysis, decides the quality of schooling? Above all, how can they maintain their professionalism?

Neither the challenges facing the profession today, nor the attacks on teachers, by those who hold political power, are themselves new. It is only just over a century ago that the first teachers' union, the National Union of Elementary Teachers, now the NUT was formed; one of the principal objects[2] of that union to 'associate and unite the teachers of England and Wales' is still relevant today, but has not yet been attained.

The need for teachers to unite to protect and advance their interests is greater than ever. But whereas the necessity for powerful teachers' unions is recognised by the vast majority of members of the profession, there is less recognition of the great weakness caused by the continued existence of separate unions. This separatism, reflected in the existence of seven associations, saps the strength of the teachers as a body of professionals which is sufficiently strong to make a powerful impact on any government's policies. What is it that separates the teachers? What are the hopes of achieving the much advocated and longed for ideal of professional unity?

The following table[3] shows the membership of the various teachers'

35

organisations as on the 1 January 1981:

Table 3.1: Membership of Teachers' Unions, July 1982

National Union of Teachers (NUT)	262,800
National Association of Schoolmasters and Union of	
Women Teachers (NAS/UWT)	119,500
Assistant Masters/Mistresses Association (AMMA)	89,100
National Association of Headteachers (NAHT)	23,700
Secondary Heads Association (SHA)	3,000
Professional Association of Teachers (PAT)	22,600
National Association of Teachers in Further and Higher	
Education (NATFHE)	73,700

Source: Figures supplied by individual unions, and published in *Times Educational Supplement*, 24 September 1982, p. 16. 'In-service membership' is given.

The National Union of Teachers

The dominance of the National Union of Teachers is at once obvious, and this is no accident. The NUT has come closest to the ideal of one all-embracing professional body, containing within its ranks teachers from all types of schools, nursery, infants, primary, middle, secondary and from all segments of the profession, from the newly qualified teacher to the heads of the large comprehensive schools. Such a diversity of membership inevitably gives rise to stresses and strains, and the NUT is certainly not free from internal conflict. In 1981, the national officers suspended one of the National Executive members – Mr Dick North, for his part in organising an unofficial strike, together with five other members of the Lambeth Local Association of the Union who were found guilty by a disciplinary panel of inciting unofficial action. Dick North has been barred from union membership for a year and banned from holding office for another 18 months.

    Within the union, primary and secondary teachers sometimes form distinct groups. Nevertheless, the NUT is recognised as the profession's main spokesman both by central government and by the local education authorities. Its policies have the hallmark of progressive educationists: it advocated the abolition of the eleven-plus examination and the introduction of comprehensive schools, a decade before the first comprehensive was created; it has consistently and successfully, opposed the attempted reintroduction of the selected schools in some areas.[4] Its advocacy of extending nursery education, of improving the quality of the emerging middle schools, its concern for the handicapped child, and its powerful case for a reform of the examination system, are part of a long tradition of widening the horizons of state education and working for the improvement of educational opportunities for the ordinary child in the ordinary school.[5]

Alongside such policies, which continue to attract and retain the loyalty and support of thousands of established teachers, the NUT provides an unrivalled range of services for its members: foremost among these are the legal departments of the Union's Headquarters, Hamilton House, London. The legal department is headed by an experienced senior solicitor working under the direction of the Law Committee of the National Executive, and has to its credit a long string of successes in protecting teachers' interests in disputes with employers, parents, private interests and public bodies. A perusal of the law reports of the National Executive indicates that the NUT has successfully dealt with the vast majority of cases concerning the tenure and conditions of service of teachers, brought actions on their behalf against libel, obtained damages in cases of assault, and generally protected its members in all kinds of professional difficulties; the legal department has developed a specialised body of knowledge in dealing with teachers cases simply not available anywhere else.[6]

Up and down the country the NUT maintains twelve regional offices, staffed by teams of full-time officials, who deal with a wide range of cases on the spot. A sample extract from the file of one of them shows an astonishing range of work being done for members in any one week: negotiating an early retirement, sorting out a redeployment problem, resisting a school closure affecting several teachers, helping a probationary teacher at risk, settling a dispute between a head and a class teacher, obtaining compensation for a teacher whose car was damaged on the school premises are all dealt with on an individual basis.

Other services offered by the NUT are no less attractive – the Teachers' Building Society provides mortgages for NUT members, and its board of unpaid directors pursues a strong policy of social landing, enabling young members to set up their first homes, with 50 per cent of all advances going to teachers under 35. The Teachers' Assurance Company offers all types of insurance policies to its members at favourable rates, and the union's 'countdown' scheme enables members to buy a wide range of goods and services up and down the country at attractive discounts. In short, the NUT member gets a lot for his relatively modest subscription of £25 per year, with a small local fee added at the discretion of the local associations, for one can only become a member of the union by joining one of them.

The NUT is organised in 558 local branches, covering all parts of the country, and varying in size from the smallest, Nidd-Valley (Yorkshire) with twelve members, to the giant Birmingham Association with 6,216 members. The local associations, or branches, are grouped into 27 divisions which are co-terminous with the areas of local education authorities. The divisional officers, all unpaid, full-time teachers, are the President, Secretary, Public Relations Officer, Treasurer, and the Teacher Representatives, who form the main negotiating team with the employers. The Presidents and Secretaries of local associations are usually teachers of considerable local standing, well known in the schools of their localities. The NUT Shop Steward is known as the school representative and is elected by the members in the schools.

The National Executive consists of 48 full-time teachers, elected bi-annually by the whole of the membership in 27 electoral districts by a system of proportional representation. The Executive meets every third or fourth week at the Union's London Headquarters, and an annual conference is held every Easter when some 2,200 delegates sit in judgment on their Executive. The NUT Annual Conference is one of the largest educational and professional gatherings in the country, and successive Secretaries of State have hardly missed the opportunity of speaking to the delegates, on occasion sometimes not without difficulty; at the 1980 conference some 200 left-wing teachers demonstrated so noisily against the then Secretary of State — Mark Carlisle, that he was unable to continue speaking, and then walked out. However, there was no doubt that the vast majority of delegates condemned their conduct as was evidenced in the support given to the President — Peter Kennedy, who strongly reprimanded them. There are many aspects of NUT policies which can and should be criticised; but its achievements over the years in protecting and advancing the causes of education have rightly raised it to the position of the major professional organisation in the country, and it has considerable standing abroad.

The National Association of Schoolmasters and Women Teachers

The National Association of Schoolmasters[7] and Union of Women Teachers (NAS/UWT) now form the second largest Teachers' Union in the country, and retain their image as an essentially separatist organisation appealing to the sometimes divergent interests of men and women teachers respectively. In earlier days, the NAS was a powerful advocate of favourable treatment for the male teachers, wanting men at a higher salary to teach boys and women to teach girls. Such a position is untenable today, and when equal pay for teachers irrespective of sex was achieved, it looked as if the real reasons for the NAS separatist existence had disappeared. Its leadership was certainly faced with a dilemma: was it to admit women teachers and so change its character and become another National Union of Teachers with a different name? The dilemma was solved, at least in the short run, by reactivating a small splinter body, the Union of Women Teachers, which had adopted a strong feminist stance by highlighting the lack of opportunities for promotion for women teachers.

The UWT became a joint partner in a new enterprise. The move saved both organisations, and the credit for this belongs to a large extent to the NAS dynamic General Secretary, Terry Casey, who provides a mixture of colourful leadership combined with an occasional stance of militancy, which appeals to many teachers. In this partnership it is the NAS Executive that makes the running. Its policy is based on the image of the strong, sometimes authoritarian teacher, pursuing essentially a traditional path of learning and of maintaining discipline. 'Six of the best' is still a medicine prescribed for dealing with ill-disciplined youngsters at NAS gatherings; a good daily dose of the three Rs and no 'truck with new-fangled progressive teaching methods' is an opinion held by many supporters of the NAS. Above all, its strong advocacy of the interests of the 'careers teacher', i.e. one whose career is not interrupted by having a family, still draws many male teachers bringing up families, and sometimes looking with displeasure or envy at the higher standards of living enjoyed by teacher couples drawing two salaries. It is not always easy to see just how the partnership with the UWT fits into this picture, and at times, the relationship has been turbulent and not a little artificial.[8] But the NAS/UWT has been skilful in seizing on issues of real discontentment within the profession; it usually opposes the NUT line in salary negotiations, tending to stick out for more money, or a different distribution; it successfully captured headlines in its opposition to a change in teachers' conditions of service, and has more than doubled its membership in less than a decade. In 1981, it was given two extra seats on the Burnham Committee which negotiates teachers' salaries, but was disappointed not to get more, leaving the NUT still in a position of majority over all other associations. As things are, it has a place as a powerful runner-up, but as the figures indicate, is a long way from the championship.

A careful study of NAS/UWT policy[9] however, reveals many points of similarity with the NUTs attitude, and it is a hopeful sign for the future that in many areas the two unions co-operate well: their representatives often vote together at meetings of the Schools Council which, although threatened with extermination, is still the major forum for professional debate in the country; they pursue generally a common policy on the Council for National Academic Award (CNAA) in the sphere of teacher education, and favour the continuation of the Bachelor of Education (B.Ed) Degree, now under challenge. In staff-rooms up and down the country, in most localities, co-operation between NUT and NAS members is good. Frequently, the local members of both organisations are critical of what they see as the mutual mud slinging by their national leaders. There is no doubt that it is much easier to achieve a united approach at places of work and in the school staffrooms than on matters of higher policy in London. Whenever either organisation has taken unilateral action against the employers, members of the others have been careful, in accordance with normal trade union practice, not to undermine such action; both the NUT and the NAS/UWT are affiliated to the TUC.

The Assistant Master and Mistresses Association and the Secondary Heads Association

The Assistant Masters and Mistresses Association (AMMA) and the Secondary Heads Association (SHA) are two relatively recent amalgamations of the previous 'Joint Four Secondary Associations' which served very largely the interests and aspirations of grammar school teachers, whilst there were many grammer schools. For many years, the four bodies were organised separately according to sex, the Assistant Masters and Assistant Mistresses as well as the Headmasters and Headmistresses owing allegiance to their own bodies, although maintaining a joint secretariat, and endeavouring to pursue joint policies in secondary education. With the progressive disappearance of grammar schools and the growth of coeducation, two developments took place; membership was open to all teachers in all types of schools; the Assistant Masters and Assistant Mistresses combined to form one union, and likewise, both male and female headteachers joined together in SHA — the Secondary Heads Association. AMMA appeals specifically to teachers who are not heads, and its policies seek to reflect the interests of class teachers; similarly, SHA is essentially for headteachers, maintaining that these have essentially specialised educational functions in school management. In this respect, both AMMA and SHAs philosophies and policies contrast sharply with the policies of the two big unions which accept both headteachers and assistants, maintaining that there should be a code of professional behaviour common to all members of the profession.

For many years, both AMMA[10] and SHA maintained reputations as organisations distinctly more moderate than either the NUT or NAS/UWT. Strikes, and indeed, any form of militant action were not favoured by the membership, but recent events, and particularly the effect of educational cuts and threats of teacher redundancy, have caused a distinct change within AMMA; thus, following the salary controversies of 1979, when the local authorities broke off negotiations, it was AMMA who, for the first time, called out its members on half-day strike, and began to change its image as an inevitably moderate teachers' organisation. Again, on many fronts, AMMA, SHA and the NUT, and sometimes the NAS/UWT, co-operate closely. There has been close agreement to reform the examination system: all unions favour a common examination at 16 plus, and co-operate in the long drawn out negotiations with reluctant governments to bring this about; the NUT, AMMA and SHA favour a reform of the GCE 'A' level examinations, and agreed on joint policies to broaden the sixth form curriculum by doing away with what they see as a narrowly based, overspecialised three subject centred curriculum, favouring five subjects taken at different levels.[11] In the field of teacher education, the unions have formed a Standing Committee and maintain a joint secretariat.

National Association of Headteachers

The 20,000 strong National Association of Headteachers (NAHT) largely organises primary school headteachers, but it is estimated that nearly a third of the members are in dual membership with either the NUT or NAS/UWT, making this organisation a less representative spokesman for the interests of school heads than its well produced literature suggests. Nationally, the NAHT makes comparatively little impact; its small membership inevitably means a small voice. Nevertheless, in many localities it brings together local heads, irrespective of their membership of other organisations, organises education forums, and makes representations on behalf of heads to local education authorities, often as part of joint machinery with the other teachers' unions.

The Professional Association of Teachers

A more recent rival to the established teachers' unions is the Professional Association of Teachers (PAT), formed specifically to attract those teachers who are against striking, whatever the issues. Its initial appeal was to teachers with a 'professional conscience', and it has succeeded in recruiting some 20,000 members, who are not only opposed to the strike weapon as such, but consider it unprofessional behaviour to take militant action of any sort under any circumstances. However, since its foundation, PAT has sometimes behaved in a bizarre manner. Its policies, apart from opposition to strike action, are not easily discernible. Whilst PAT scored a victory in 1981 by gaining admission to the Burnham Committee as a result of a ruling given by Mark Carlisle, the Conservative Secretary of State for Education, and can thus claim to have achieved in a couple of years what took the NAS 40 years to achieve, it is not a serious contender for power within the profession at present. Nor is it likely to grow, as present government policies drive teachers towards militancy rather than moderation.

National Association of Teachers in Higher and Further Education

The chief partner of the NUT is the National Association of Teachers in Further and Higher Education (NATFHE) which organises the teaching force throughout the post-school sector, other than in the universities. NATFHE has virtually a monopoly of membership in further education and technical colleges and in Polytechnics, and among lecturers in the teacher training establishments, where some years ago it absorbed the Association of Teachers in Departments of Education (ATDE). NATFHE and the NUT work in close harness; there is no competitive recruitment; the headquarters of both organisations are in the same building, and there is cross representation between the two national executives. However, there are occasional differences on some vital issues: their respective attitudes to the education of the 16-19 age group is one of them: many NUT members maintain a policy in favour of school-based sixth forms, though not opposed to tertiary colleges for the 16-19 age group in certain localities. Accepting that such a tertiary solution is appropriate in some areas, the majority of NUT secondary teachers still strongly favour the 11-18 comprehensive school with its own sixth form, whereas NATFHE has firmly nailed its colours to the mast of a break of 16 plus, to the dismay of the NUT. Negotiations to overcome certain strains are part of a continuous dialogue in what has always been a fruitful partnership. The Macfarlane Report,[12] leaving it to the localities to decide on the shape of post-school education, is seen as a useful compromise enabling both the NATFHE and the NUT to maintain flexible policies in the 16–19 sector.

Whatever the differences between the various teachers' unions, their community of interests clearly outweigh the reasons for a continued separate existence. Karl Marx once urged the working classes: 'Proletarians of the world, unite, you have nothing to lose but your chains.' Today, the teachers of Britain need urging: 'Teachers of Britain unite, you have everything to lose if you don't.' Many new entrants to the profession are both bewildered and disillusioned by the lack of unity among teachers, but how is this unity to be achieved? What issues of substance still separate teachers into seven different professional organisations, and thereby weaken their power and their influence at a time when they are with their backs to the wall, fighting redundancy and growing threats of teacher unemployment? What practical steps can and should be taken to bring about a strong, united teaching profession? Anyone who has ever stood in a classroom or sat in a staffroom, knows that within the school environment, many of the issues which appear to divide teachers at their union headquarters are of little significance in day-to-day school life. However, one major difference on which strongly held opinions lead to division, is the attitude to strikes. Should teachers strike? Is professionalism compatible with striking, given that the people who suffer are the children who are the innocent party, whatever the cause of dispute between teachers and their employers, or between teachers and the government? In any case, what have teachers' strikes achieved and what are they likely to achieve in the future?

Teachers' Strikes

There has never been a general teachers' strike. Although the strike weapon has been used, the occasions have been far and few between. The history of teacher politics[13] contains fascinating accounts of an unofficial strike in the Rhondda led by W.G. Cove, who later became a well known member of parliament, and in Lowestoft and Gateshead in the 1920s. These strikes took place because the local education authorities in the areas affected refused to pay what the teacher thought was their due at a time when salaries were negotiated locally.

In 1931, the Geddes Axe cut teachers' pay by 10 per cent, but no strikes of any significance took place. In the post-war periods there have been several instances when large scale teachers' strikes seemed imminent, but in the end did not happen. Curiously enough, one of the most successful militant stands the teachers made was in 1950 when the Labour controlled Durham County Council attempted to enforce the closed shop and insisted that every teacher in its service should join a union.[14] All the teachers' unions were opposed to this policy, supporting the principle of maintaining the freedom not to join a union as something worth fighting for. Some 5,000 resignation notices were collected, an interesting variant from the normal strike procedure: the teachers said that they would rather not work for a local authority which bullied them into compulsory unionism, and the employers were faced with mass resignations which would certainly have brought the schools of Durham to a halt had they taken effect. In the event, the teachers won the day.

Recently, strike action has taken place more frequently, but usually only for relatively short periods. Only the NUT and the NAS/UWT have called their members out on strike, apart from one half-day strike called by AMMA in 1979. Such strikes have generally been highly selective and have been organised on an area basis. In the last two years, there have been short strikes, usually half a day, or a day, in Avon, Trafford and Inner London; the NUT conducted a highly successful ten week strike in Barking (a Labour controlled authority) against the local authority's attempt to dismiss 90 teachers, and won the day.[15] The union with the greatest clout, the NUT, has a rule requiring each school to ballot its members and to register a two-thirds majority before strike action can take place and money paid out of its sustentation fund. In addition, the action committee of the NUTs Executive is required to approve any strike action before it takes off, even if there is the required majority. Thus, a tight grip is maintained by the leaders on unofficial strikes of the kind prevalent in some industries. The suspension of Dick North, a London Member of the National Executive, and leader of the Lambeth teachers, together with the officers of the Lambeth Association, highlighted the leadership's determination to stay at the helm. North and the Lambeth officers voted to support strike action called by other unions, but failed to obtain the approval of the National Action Committee. The strike went ahead nevertheless, and was followed by the suspension of North who is one of the leaders of a radical, left-wing movement within the NUT known as 'Rank and File'. Though small in number (it contains some 2,000–3,000 teachers who support it regularly) it provides a challenge to the leadership which is supported mainly by young teachers, and it is certainly a significant ginger group which is always in evidence at national conferences. It publishes 'Rank and File'; regularly attacks the NUT Executive on all issues ranging from salary policy to its supposed lack of willingness to take strong militant action, and sees itself as the spokesman for the underdog, the class teacher on Scale 1. School heads are seen as the main enemies, having no place in the NUT; the political neutrality of the NUT is attacked as one of its weaknesses, as Rank and File stands for an alliance of teachers with trade unionists, and favours schools being run by committees of class teachers, students and ancillary staffs. Rank and File has some support in London, in the Midlands and the North, and some 30 local associations, especially in London, have officers and committees well known as Rank and File supporters. Resolutions calling for strike action are the order of the day in such associations, and there is little doubt that many moderate NUT members have been alienated by what they see as extreme and politically inspired policies. Some Rank and File members are known to be active members of the Socialist Workers Party; others are said to belong to small revolutionary groups. Sometimes, their language is the language of political programmes somewhat removed from the classroom. At the Union's Annual Conference, Rank and File promotes resolutions, holds meetings, distributes pamphlets and frequently succeeds in getting its speakers to the rostrum. However, when resolutions or amendments supported by the movement, are put to the vote, they are usually lost by overwhelming majorities. The existence of the Rank and File movement within the NUT, is not only tolerated but seen by many moderate members as a sign of democratic strength, the ability to contain a dissident element and accord to it the right of freedom of speech. The large body of NUT membership remains essentially moderate, and this is clearly reflected in the reluctance of the NUT to take strike action. Both the NAS/UWT and AMMA follow similar policies, involving careful consultation with local members, including the taking of ballots indicating the likely success which might be achieved if a strike were called, and generally avoiding a situation where schools are closed because of strikes. The general picture which emerges is that of a highly disciplined profession, acting within the rules of its unions, and not lightly engaging in unofficial action. There is clear evidence[16] that hard negotiations take place at local level, and teachers' negotiators have a reputation for being both patient and persistent, often achieving their objectives in the face of considerable difficulties.

School Meals Sanctions

Apart from strike weapons, other sanctions have from time to time been used: one of the most effective, and also one of the most controversial, is the withdrawal of teachers from supervising the midday meal. This was used during the 1979 salary dispute and created considerable disruption. By agreement with the employers, meals supervision is voluntary for class teachers, although headteachers have legal responsibilities to ensure the safety of pupils, which put them in a very difficult position when teachers withdraw from supervising. Since a head cannot divest himself of this responsibility, he is sometimes the only person on the school premises to supervise pupils during the lunch hour. The impact on a school community where large numbers stay for school lunch and cannot reach their homes within a short time, can be considerable if teachers decide to withdraw. If school meals continue to be served when there are no teachers to supervise, discipline deteriorates dramatically, and the few ancillary helpers employed in schools cannot effectively supervise without the authority of the teachers behind them. If children bring sandwiches and eat them on the school premises, the need for supervision still remains; if sandwiches are not allowed, all pupils must leave the school premises and may not, and often, because of the distance involved, cannot, return for the afternoon session, and as a result lessons are disrupted. It is significant that even at a time of severe retrenchment, only one local education authority — Dorset, has done away with the school meals service. Others have introduced cafeteria systems, raised their prices, but maintained the meals service as an integral part of the school day, continuing to rely on the teachers to supervise. Some secondary schools faced chaos when this supervision was withdrawn in 1979. There is no doubt that such a withdrawal is an effective weapon which teachers can, and do, employ.

'No Cover' Action

Another powerful sanction used by the teachers is 'no cover action'. This means that a teacher will refuse to take lessons for a colleague who is absent, thereby forcing the authority to employ supply teachers over and above what is normally allowed. In most areas, three days have to elapse before a supply teacher is allowed, and secondary teachers are expected to cover classes for absent colleagues by giving up their non-teaching time. In primary schools more often than not classes are split, or the head or deputy head has to teach full time. During the last two years, 'no cover action' has been used successfully in a number of areas:

in 1979, the Avon Authority cut £4 million from its education budget, involving the reduction of its teaching force by the equivalent of 300 full-time teachers. No cover action and token strikes resulted in only four teachers losing their jobs. In Bexley, Kent, the inadequate numbers of supply teachers being provided was substantially increased as a result of no cover action. Similar successes were achieved in Brent, in Bromley, Essex, Newcastle and Newham. Thus, at a time when redundancies were taking place both in the private sector and public service, including redundancies amongst other educational workers, the teachers have very largely held the line, and by the Spring of 1981, no teacher, other than Eileen Crosbie, had been sacked. There is no doubt that no cover action has played a substantial part in maintaining this position.

Other sanctions, including the withdrawal from extra curricular activities, a refusal to attend staff meetings or parent/teacher meetings after school, advocated mainly by NAS/UWT, have proved unpopular, and had relatively little following in staffrooms. The NAS/UWT also attempted on one occasion to use what could be a very powerful weapon; it asked its members to consider withdrawal from any duties connected with invigilating public examinations. However, the NUT set its face firmly against what it considered irresponsible action which would have hit particular pupils at a vital stage of their school careers, and the NAS/UWT, without NUT support, never carried out its threat.

Redundancy

But having been successful in warding off large scale redundancy so far is no reason for complacency. In fact, the threat of teachers getting the sack is considerably greater during 1982 and 1983 than in the late 1970s or 1980 or 1981. The government's spending plans, if followed to the letter, mean a loss of 29,000 teachers' jobs in 1983, or 40,000 jobs unless pay settlements are under 6 per cent. This projection includes 25,000 compulsory redundancies by September 1983, and a worsening of the overall pupil/teacher ratio from 18.8 to 19.8. Only some 9,000 teachers are expected to retire early, or leave through natural wastage, during the same periods. The threat of the sack is certainly there, but must be seen with a sense of proportion: the very group which produced the figures, and this includes DES officials and LEA representatives, also concludes that a cut of 40,000 jobs is 'virtually impossible'; it would not only seriously affect the curriculum, but is also seen, no doubt, as politically risky – hence Sir Keith Joseph's recent idea to give local authorities freedom to pay teachers more than the statutory redundancy payments for public service workers to encourage 'voluntary redundancy', hardly known among teachers under 50 years of age. The LEAs calculate that they need an extra £510 million for 1983 to enable them to maintain present policies — a gradual run-down of the size of the teaching force, rather than the drama of sackings. The DES puts the figure at £394 million. The likelihood is that there will be some redundancies but looking at trends, the writer suggests that the figure is more likely to be around 10,000 with considerable variations locally, areas with quickly falling rolls being particularly vulnerable. Whatever the figure, it is highly probable that confrontations between individual LEAs and teachers will increase in intensity and frequency in the next two or three years.

What then are the hopes for the teachers' unions in meeting the threats of redundancy? It is evident that the vast majority of teachers are extremely reluctant to use the strike method for a number of reasons: first and foremost, the teachers see themselves as professionals, working for and with the children, and are keenly aware that striking harms their pupils. This attitude inevitably causes a dilemma; if teachers are made redundant and class sizes increase, if teachers neither qualified nor able to teach certain subjects are forced to do so by cuts in staffing, the children suffer. Therefore, in order to protect the interests of the children as much as the teachers, some action is necessary. If employers will not listen to arguments and accelerate a policy of sacking, what is left for the teachers to do but strike? But how successful would such a strike be, bearing in mind that when teachers strike they actually save their employers money, a sharp contrast with the situation which pertains in industry? Teachers' salaries are inevitably the largest item of expenditure in the educational budget. For every day on which teachers strike, the local education authorities save millions of pounds and both teachers and employers are only too well aware of this. Then there is the attitude of parents: it is one thing for parents to support teachers in their opposition to education cuts; it is quite another to be sure of parental support when children are unable to go to school, and when parents themselves have sometimes been the victims of redundancy. Such considerations make it extremely unlikely that large scale strikes will take place, even at a time of severe cuts in educational expenditure. The teachers are much more likely to continue to rely on no cover action, and in particular, on mobilising public opinion against the policy of cuts. Here, some teachers can claim considerable success: in Norfolk, a proposed cut of £5½ million from the 1981 budget of £121 million, was reduced to £2½ million after an intensive publicity campaign involving hundreds of parents, public meetings, deputations to county councillors, lobbying meetings of the council, and gaining considerable publicity on the media and in the press. In many parts of the county, parent/teacher associations have sided with the teachers in opposing the cuts. The action of national bodies such as the Confederation for the Advancement of State Education (CASE), the National Federation of Parent/Teacher Associations, shows very clearly that the organised body of parents recognise the identity of interests of teachers and children; however, such parental support usually stops short once strikes take place.

However, the present frustrations felt within the professions should not be underestimated: alongside a feeling of relief shown by many teachers that they are still in receipt of a monthly salary, there is a tremendous and widespread feeling of burning injustice against the cuts, against continuous teacher bashing by politicians. This is particularly strong among the young and lower paid teachers, who see little hope of promotion, find it difficult to move to another area, and witness the deteriorating conditions in schools, whether it is by not replacing much needed textbooks or not having enough equipment to teach properly; there is a great deal of bitterness in staffrooms. We may not see a prolonged teachers' strike on a national scale with thousands of schools closed, and tens of thousands of children on the streets all over the country, but we are likely to see, in the next few years, frequent no cover action based on individual schools, or groups of schools, periodic withdrawals from parent/teacher meetings, and other post-school functions, refusals to teach oversized classes, and short, sharp strikes in those areas where sackings are attempted. These will occur alongside long-term continuous efforts to influence public opinion against the cuts in educational expenditure.

Teacher Representatives

Locally, the teachers have one powerful weapon which they use to good effect: nearly all education committees of local education authorities contain teacher representatives, and the vast majority of these are elected by their unions. The teachers are unique among local government employees in having direct representations on the policy making bodies of the employers. In the majority of areas the National Union of Teachers dominates, and sometimes occupies all the seats accorded to teachers on education committees. The number of teacher representatives varies between two and six, usually representing the primary and secondary sectors, and the further education interest. In other areas, as in Norfolk, an understanding is reached between the unions, and there is a sharing out of the available seats before the local elections, so that teachers act in unison, whatever their union allegiance. The legal requirement on local education authorities is simply that they should co-opt a proportion of teacher representatives onto their education committees, though how this is done and who is co-opted is left to each authority. It is to the credit of local education authorities that the vast majority have regard to the democratic principle and co-opt only those teachers elected by their unions. There are regrettably, however, still a few cases where local authorities simply select an individual teacher who represents nobody but himself; the practice is lessening as it is recognised that people answerable to nobody often speak for nobody, and are therefore, not much use. Teachers are, however, barred from offering themselves for election as candidates of political parties, or independent candidates, in the counties in which they are employed, and in that sense, their civic rights are less than those of other citizens. To some extent, representation on education committees is therefore seen as a compensation for the teachers' inability to contest local elections in those areas in which they work; this is resented by teachers, and the issues of civic rights for them often figure prominently on the agenda of their union conferences.

Together with other co-opted members of education committees, notably those representing the churches, sometimes the universities, industry and commerce, the teachers form a powerful element within a group which is politically uncommitted, and can carry considerable weight in committees, especially when no political party enjoys an absolute majority. The attitude of the elected representatives of the political parties towards co-opted teacher members varies: some court them, but others challenge the right of the teachers to be there at all, though most councillors accept that the teachers, being in school every day, know what they are talking about. Since education committees are usually open to both public and press, the teachers' pronouncements often attract considerable attention, and their spokesmen appear on local television and radio whenever there is a live local issue, such as school closures. In the eyes of the public, teacher representatives have one great advantage over politicians: they are not committed to a party, cannot aspire to political office, and are therefore seen, particularly by parents, as genuinely standing for the educational interests of a locality, whatever the prevailing party line. This gives them a position of considerable strength. Minutes of education committees and reports from up and down the country indicate very clearly that teachers have frequently lessened the impacts of proposed cuts on the education service, have been successful in preventing teacher redundancies, and have mobilised public opinion for a particular local cause; indeed, it is not uncommon for members of the ruling political party to express privately support for the teachers case whilst, at the same time, publicly following the party line.

Joint Consultative Committees

Apart from direct participation in the affairs, and voting as full members of education committees, a network of joint consultative and joint advisory committees between the teachers and local councillors exists in all areas. These JCCs usually contain the leading members of the local education authorities as well as those of the teachers' unions. Thus, the Norfolk JCC is chaired by the chairman of the education committee, the vice-chairman is a teacher, and the divisional NUT secretary and chief education officer act as joint secretaries, carrying equal status. Several prominent members of the county council, including the education committee's vice-chairman, the chairman of sub-committees, join the representatives of the NUT, NAS/UWT, AMMA, NAHT, NATFHE and SHA (though not PAT)[17] with the NUT having an overall majority. The issues coming up for decision in the education committee are frequently first discussed in the JCC, which not only provides a useful sounding board for both employers and teachers, but enables both sides to see the drift of policies and the likely sticking points. Private meetings between the officers of the council and the teachers, and frequently between the chairman of education committee and the teacher representatives, often take place to deal with sensitive issues. Thus, in Norfolk, an agreement whereby teachers sought to obtain a guarantee that there would be no redundancies providing they co-operated fully in redeployment procedures, provided a working formula which has so far avoided redundancies. The teachers, by their inolvement in the political process without membership of a political party, thus play a considerable part in the governmental process at local level.

Parliamentary Links

Although there are a considerable number of ex-teachers in the House of Commons, the influence of the teachers unions in parliament is less strong. The NUT maintains parliamentary links through the union's consultants, and there are at present, four MPs, Mr Ernest Armstrong,[18] Mr G. Barnett, Mr M. Flannery (who has himself been a member of the NUT Executive), and Mr B. Jones, who act as parliamentary consultants

when educational matters are being debated; when an educational bill
is dealt with, the teachers send deputations to meet MPs and frequently
give evidence before select committees. But the diversity of interests
of members of parliament and the nature of the parliamentary process,
favours teacher influence rather less than in the localities, and although
rows with ministers gain headlines in the press, the teachers' lobby,
whilst surfacing at times of crisis, is perhaps not the strongest. A closer
relationship exists between the Unions and the Department of Education and Science. Both the Senior Inspector and the Senior Civil
Servants frequently meet teachers' deputations, attend teachers conferences, serve on joint consultative committees, and provide a network
of professional contacts.

The Schools Council

Indeed, it is in the educational sphere that the unions take on the
character of professional associations. Most major issues of educational
policies of concern to teachers — class sizes, curriculum development,
examination reform, in-service training, the methodology of teaching,
parent/teacher relations, relations between headteachers and class
teachers, are covered by the education departments of the major
unions who also provide the organised teachers with an effective voice
in the main forums where educational policy is discussed and decided.
Among these the Schools Council is the most important. Professional
associations are represented roughly in proportion to their membership;
teachers achieve prominent positions as committee chairmen and the
present acting chairman of the council, Arnold Jennings, was a distinguished headteacher. A decade ago their position was even stronger, one
of the posts of joint secretaries being held by a teacher. Since the re-
constitution of the Schools Council in 1977, the teachers have lost
some ground, and other interests — local education authorities, industry
and commerce, the parents, and particularly the Department of Education and Science, are more strongly represented. However, this has also
enabled the teachers to participate and make their influence felt in a
wider forum, and it is significant that the Schools Council has adopted
a generally progressive stance; thus, in a debate on the government's
interventionism in curricular matters, the Council has declared that it
considers itself a better instrument than the Department of Education
and Science to pronounce on matters of curriculum, because it is
widely representative and includes the professional interests. In the
present movement towards reforming the 16 plus examination, to
which both the Labour and the Conservative party are now committed,

the Council has relied heavily on its teacher members to chart the way. The three main components of the Schools Council are Convocation, containing representatives of all professional associations, of parents, industry and commerce, the local authorities, the Department of Education and Science and the universities; the Professional Committee, on which the teachers have a majority, and the Finance and Priorities Committee, which is controlled by the local education authorities. The representatives of the various teachers' unions act in accord and provide the kind of example of professional unity which is so badly needed at the present time. There may be differences of approach and of emphasis, but by and large co-operation is good.

The Conservative government elected in 1979 was acutely conscious of the Schools Council's progressive stance, and the prominent part played by the teachers' unions in its affairs. In 1981, the Prime Minister invited Nancy Trenaman, Principal of St Anne's College, Oxford, to carry out a thorough review of its purpose, functioning and constitution. The review criticised the elaborate committee structure of the council, the powerful influence of the unions, and recommended a smaller, less elaborate body — but in essence, the Council was seen as a valuable educational body, whose continued existence was recommended without reservation. Sir Keith Joseph has disregarded this recommendation and has made his intention clear to abolish it, and replace it by two small, separate bodies, one to oversee the curriculum, the other to deal with examinations. Both bodies are to consist of persons nominated by the Secretary of State himself, and not by the various educational and other interests who now elect members to the Schools Council. The absurdity of having two bodies dealing with the interdependent and closely related issues of curriculum and examinations has been widely condemned in educational circles, but the motive for this action is not, of course, educational, but political. It is, on the one hand, an attack on the teachers' professionalism, a cynical disregard for their views, their expertise, and their professional organisations; on the other, it is a clear, decisive move towards centralised decision making in the educational process, with the Secretary of State seeing himself as the powerful all-knowing leviathan, who can afford to ignore democratic processes, and steamroll schools, parents, teachers, and above all children, in the direction he chooses. Such methods, in a free society, have never stood the test of time. A new vigorous School Council may well emerge from the ashes of the present one, in a different political climate.

Union co-operation is evident in other educational bodies. On the Council of National Academic Awards, NUT and NAS/UWT members sit side by side, participate in evaluating proposals for B.Ed and M.Ed degrees and bring a wealth of professional experience to the deliberations of its Committee for Education and to the working parties visiting institutes of teacher education and polytechnics. In the course of a decade, there have hardly been any differences of view on matters relating to teacher education.

The Examinations Boards

The bodies conducting the major public examinations, the GCE Boards and the CSE Boards, also rely very heavily on the teachers, and would be unable to function without them. Whilst there is some feeling in the profession that certain GCE Boards are often dominated by university interests, the boards have independent legal status and are not answerable either to the Department of Education and Science, or to the teachers. Secretaries and senior officials of GCE Boards occupy powerful positions, are often the initiators of examination policy, and have a major influence on resource allocation. The teachers have a large say in the examining process and in determining the details of the examination, and of course, act as examiners, but are there largely in an individual capacity; union representation is less strong and this can mean that some teachers who serve on the policy-making bodies of the GCE Boards are accountable to nobody but themselves.

The CSE Boards, on the other hand, are teacher controlled, though in the proposals for the reform of the examination system, this control is being challenged both by the government and the local education authorities. At present, the governing bodies of all CSE Boards have constitutions which give teachers representation according to union strength; local education authorities and other interests are represented, but the teachers have the majority. Representatives report back to their unions and policy thus takes account of grass-roots opinion and professional consensus.

How then can teachers move further and faster towards professional unity? It is an idle hope that this will come overnight, in spite of the tremendous crisis which the education service faces. Attitudes are too deeply entrenched and organisational forms too rigid to make radical change possible. However, what can be done and needs to be done quickly, is to move purposefully towards a federal structure. The NUT, at its recent annual conferences, has passed motions instructing their executive to pursue a policy towards professional unity, and this movement is likely to become stronger in the next decade. The NUT and NATFHE already have a partnership which eliminates competitive recruitment. This is a model which must be extended to all teachers' associations as such. The formation of a Joint Standing Committee, where the different unions sit down together and seriously thrash out what still divides them is long overdue. Certainly, leaders of teachers' associations sometimes underestimate the strong desire which one finds in staffrooms for one body who speaks for all teachers. The antagonisms between general secretaries and sometimes between national executives of the different unions are seldom reflected in staffrooms. As rolls fall, school closures increase, security of tenure disappears and jobs fall by the wayside, separatism among teachers will be as outdated as the horse and cart. The need is for imaginative leadership bringing about, first, a federation of all teachers' unions which can speak with one voice on those issues on which there is no dissent, namely resistance to the educational cuts and to the policy of large scale school closures, to teacher redundancy and to a worsening of conditions of service. From such a federation, one body representing all teachers can and should develop. The NUT has managed to contain in its ranks a diversity of professional interests: class teachers and headteachers, nursery, primary and secondary teachers, the three-year certificated and the first class honours graduate, the newly qualified and the teachers about to retire, and indeed, those who have retired, are all to be found at local association meetings. There is every reason why this model should be followed throughout the profession. This need not mean NUT domination. There are issues on which the NUT needs to show greater sensitivity and greater flexibility than it has done in the past. But as the largest, the most powerful and the most representative body of teachers, it is clearly in the best position to provide the foundation on which unity must be built. Differences will continue to exist, but can be lessened and often resolved within the framework of one union for all teachers. This is how teacher unionism started in the 1870s, when elementary education became the right of every child. This right is now under threat, and the profession needs to respond by putting its own house in order.

Notes

1. For an account of the work of the Assessment of Performance Unit (APU), see Chapter six.
2. 'Objects', NUT Annual Report for 1981, p. 14.
3. Teachers, especially heads, are sometimes in dual membership; for example, heads may belong to both NAHT and NUT.
4. The Kent Local Authority attempted to do this in 1979 in Erith, but was

not successful. In Worcester, there is a scheme to bring back a grammar school.

5. For accounts of the history of the NUT, see *The Growth of the Teaching Profession* by A. Tropp (Heinemann, London, 1959). *The Teachers' Union* by W. Roy (Schoolmaster Publishing Company, London, 1968).

6. See Reports of Law Committee in NUT Annual Reports, NUT, Hamilton House Library, London.

7. The NAS was founded in 1922, when some 2,000 teachers in the NUT disagreed with its policy of advocating equal pay for women teachers, and decided to form their own union.

8. Usually, the NAS makes the running and gets the publicity.

9. In salary negotiations, however, there are often differences – see Chapter four.

10. Throughout the 1970s, AMMA appeared to be gaining ground at the expense of both the NUT and the NAS/UWT, with moderate teachers joining it. This movement appears to have halted since the founding of PAT, the Professional Teachers' Association.

11. Various proposals, including the ill-fated Schools Council proposals to establish N and F examinations to replace 'A' levels, have been mooted during the last 20 years; none has come to fruition.

12. See Macfarlane Report (HMSO, London, 1981).

13. Especially A. Tropp's account in *The Growth of the Teaching Profession* (Heineman, London, 1959) and the NUT Annual Reports.

14. *The Teachers' Union* by W. Roy (Schoolmaster Publishing Company, London, 1968). Chapter five contains a full account of the Durham dispute.

15. During the last two years, no cover or strike action has taken place in Kent, Leicestershire, Lincolnshire, Northamptonshire, Staffordshire, Surrey, Sutton, Trafford, Nottinghamshire.

16. NUT Annual Reports and the educational press give details of local negotiations week by week.

16a. It has to be said that teachers still enjoy more protection against redundancy than many other workers. National agreements give certain safeguards when reorganisation of schools take place. The strength of teachers' unions, and public sympathy for education all play a part in maintaining a relatively high degree of protection. However, circumstances vary in the localities: a teacher employed by the Inner London Education Authority usually finds herself in a more favourable position than one working in a conservative controlled shire bent on cutting staffing establishments.

17. However, there are increasing signs that PAT is gaining representation on a number of local committees, in spite of the opposition of the established teachers' organisations.

18. Ernest Armstrong, is now Deputy Speaker and will cease to be a consultant.

4 PAY AND CONDITIONS OF SERVICE

How well are teachers paid compared with others with similar qualifications and length of training? How valid are such comparisons? What factors determine teachers' pay and how do they relate to conditions of service? What can teachers expect to earn in the 1980s?

Table 4.4 in Appendix I sets out in full the present salary scales of teachers, which includes 6 per cent awarded in June, 1982 by an arbitration body following a breakdown of negotiations. Teachers progress through five salary scales — Scale 1 to Senior teacher — from a minimum of £4,932 per annum to £12,141 for Senior Teachers; increments are paid each September for 13 years, with special allowances for good honours graduates on Scale 1, 'merit' additions for specialist qualifications, and extra allowances for those teaching in the London area, and in the social priority schools — an allowance now disappearing. But the salary tables tell us very little beyond the factual information; for teachers to evaluate their prospects, a more detailed picture of the distribution of who gets what money is needed. This is shown in Table 4.1:

Table 4.1: Distribution of Pay Between Salary Scales

Teachers	£4,932 to £12,141	through five scales
Heads	£8,676 to £20,793	pay depends on size
Deputy Heads	£6,168 to £15,126	of school

32% of teachers earn below £7,755 (the top of Scale 1)
64% of teachers earn below £8,700 (the top of Scale 2)
79% of teachers earn below £9,999 (the top of Scale 3)
85% of teachers earn below £11,205 (the top of Scale 4)

Source: Figures supplied by the National Union of Teachers Salaries Department, based on April 1982 Salary Scales.

The average teacher earns £7,645 per annum, and is on point 9 on Scale 2, and 7 per cent of teachers are deputy heads and 7 per cent are headteachers.

Teachers' Pay Settlements

John Hughes,[1] an acknowledged authority on teachers' pay, and usually the teachers' nominee when arbitration takes place, points out that before the Houghton award in 1974, the average pay of men teachers in primary and secondary schools in England and Wales was 3 per cent less than that of non-manual males. Houghton added 24 per cent; following the Clegg award which added 18 per cent, the same teachers were still 6 per cent behind the normal worker in 1979. Teachers' pay has not only not kept up with inflation, but has fallen behind that of white collar workers as a group. Pay settlements in recent years bear this out; although the Clegg award in 1979 achieved a betterment factor, this has largely been lost, as is shown in Table 4.2.

Table 4.2: Pay Settlements, 1976–82

1976/7:	£6 a week (basic Incomes Policy)
1977/8:	£2.50/£4.00 a week formula (basic Incomes Policy)
1978/9:	10% (basic Incomes Policy)
1979/80:	9.3% from 1 April 1979 plus 17% to 25%, half from 1 January 1980 and half from 1 September 1980 (This equals an average of 29.2 per cent spread over 18 months) (Clegg Award)
1980/1:	12% from 1 April 1980 plus 2½% to 4% from 1.9.80
1981/2:	7¾% from 1 April 1981 plus promise of working party to review salary structure
1982/3:	6% from April, 1982

Source: Figures supplied by the National Union of Teachers Salaries Department.

Allowing for the 6 per cent superannuation deduction, health insurance payments, and average tax commitments, the average take home pay is about £120 to £130 per week.

Given present government policies on curbing pay in the public sector, the application of cash limits to local authorities, and threat to many teachers' jobs whenever any increase is paid, the outlook is not good. Unless this policy can be reversed, overall pay levels in the early and mid-1980s will undoubtedly be largely determined by continued severe restraints on pay in the public sector, tempered by such resistance as the teachers are able to muster. There is no doubt that both LEAs and the government want fewer teachers, and less money spent on the salary bill, whatever the problems of distribution between different scales. But it is not only current government policy as such, but the impact of falling rolls in schools that is the most serious threat to a real improvement of teachers' pay. In their evidence to the Clegg[2] Commission, the Management Panel of the Burnham Committee, representing the local authorities, laid considerable stress on market forces; they said that at the time of the Houghton award in 1974, there had been widespread problems in recruiting and retaining teachers. These problems, they stated, had largely disappeared; apart from particular shortages in individual subjects, notably mathematics and physics, there was an over-supply of teachers. Professor Briault, in a penetrating study of the effect of falling rolls in schools on job prospects, the curriculum and school organisation[3] argues strongly for a change in the Burnham system of settling pay, and other authorities[4] support his arguments.

Houghton and Clegg Awards

The major influences on Pay in the 1970s were the Houghton Award and the Clegg Report.[5] Both bodies were set up following the inability of the teachers and their employers to agree – an inability which has been the hallmark of salary negotiations throughout the 1970s, in contrast to agreed settlements in the stable period of the 1950s and 1960s. Twice within five years, in 1974 and again in 1979, special mahinery has had to be set up following breakdowns in negotiations; in annual salary negotiations since 1969, there have only been three negotiated settlements – in 1969, 1973 and 1974. Since then, teachers' pay has been determined either by the government's pay policy or by arbitration awards.

John Hughes reminds us that in the run up to the Houghton Award in 1974, high wastage and high staff turnover were serious symptoms of the decline in salary levels. Houghton recommended a 16 per cent increase at the bottom of the scale and 32 per cent at the top for a few heads of large schools, with an average of 24 per cent, but found his recommendation reversed by the 1975 arbitration award. This raised the Scale 1 teacher by 34 per cent, and the heads at the top of the scale by 17 per cent, and gave an overall increase of 22.3 per cent. Clegg widened the differential again with 17 per cent at the bottom and 25 per cent at the top. Houghton spoke of salary levels being 'reasonably favourable' at the beginning, but said that 'chances of earning high salaries later' were more limited. Since 1974, they have been severely limited at either end! Clegg carried out an elaborate exercise establishing a list of comparators, seeking to slot teaching into some pecking

Table 4.3: Teachers Pay Settlements, 1969–80

Date	Percentage Increase	Remarks
1 April 1969	7.1	Negotiated settlement
1 April 1970	7.5	Flat rate increase (£120 p.a. increase for all teachers)
1 April 1971	10.8	Arbitration Award: New Scale structure introduced
1 April 1972	9.6	Arbitration Award
1 April 1973	6.6	Negotiated settlement
1 April 1974	8.0	Negotiated settlement
24 May 1974	27.0	Houghton Award – estimated to be worth 29.0% in the long term
1 April 1975	22.3	Arbitration Award: Included consolidation of threshold payments in payment since June, 1974
1 April 1976	8.3	£6 p.w. pay policy
1 April 1977	3.8	£2.50/5%/£4.00 p.w. pay policy
1 April 1978	9.9	10% pay policy
1 April 1979	9.3	Plus £6 p.w. 'on account' and reference to Standing Commission on Pay Comparability
	17–25	Clegg findings Av. increase – 18.2% Award in 2 parts 1.1.80 and 1.9.80
1 April 1980	13.5	Arbitration Award 12% All salaries 2–4½% – widening Differentials as from 1.9.80

Source: Figures supplied by NUT Salaries Department.

order of civil servants, local government officers, groups of professional and white collar workers generally and seeking to set up a series of 'benchmarks'. The exercise was a disastrous failure; the description of tasks performed, length of training, working conditions, nature of the work made meaningful comparison impossible; the ranking was acknowledged to be subjective even by the panels, which included teachers, who understood the task, although Clegg succeeded in establishing criteria whereby graduate entrants to teaching would not, after three years, be seriously out of line with salary levels for similar graduates in industry and commerce. The facts indicate that no satisfactory way of comparing teachers salaries with that of other occupational groups exists.

What then, does determine pay levels? In the final analysis, it is the relative strength of the opposing forces, and in particular, the government's willingness, or lack of it, to find the money, and this is in turn, influenced by the negotiations which take place, each year, between teachers and the local authorities. What then happens inside the Burnham Committee once the various parties sit, if not round a table, at least in the same room?

The Burnham Committee

The Burnham Committee[6] consists of some 63 people. The employers' side, the management panel, is made up of the representatives of the local education authorities: the association of county councils, the association of metropolitan authorities, and the Welsh Joint Education Committee; on the other side are ranged the spokesmen for the teachers' organisations: The National Union of Teachers has half the 32 seats, and is joined by representatives of the National Association of Schoolmasters and Union of Women Teachers (NAS/UWT), the Association of Assistant Masters and Mistresses (AMMA), the Secondary Heads Associations (SHA), the National Association of Headteachers (NAHT), the National Association of Higher and Further Education (NATFHE), and the recently admitted Professional Association of Teachers (PAT). There is an independent chairman appointed by the government and the Department of Education and Science provides two assessors.

It is this large body which meets usually for several days to consider the claims put forward annually by the teachers and whose deliberations usually result in a breakdown. Why is there this breakdown?

First, there is the need for the representatives of the teachers' organisations to agree exactly what the claims should be, and this has proved to be no easy matter. It is one of the weaknesses of the teaching profession that it is not united, and its lack of unity is reflected in the claims put forward by the separate organisation. Those claiming to represent the heads – NAHT and SHA – usually want special treatment for school heads; the NAS/UWT always follows a distinctly individualistic approach staking its own claim. If no agreement between the teachers' organisations is reached, a vote is taken, and since the National Union of Teachers, with NATFHE, has the majority, it is inevitably the NUT view which prevails. The claim is then presented by the leader of the teachers' panel, who is Fred Jarvis, the General Secretary of the NUT.

A similar procedure is followed on the other side of the table. The local authorities meet in private before any negotiation takes place, and endeavour to agree amongst themselves how much they are prepared to pay. Their attitude depends on two factors: one is the current political composition of the Management Panel: the Association of County Councils is usually dominated by conservative politicians; the Association of Metropolitan Authorities is more often than not labour controlled, though in the last three years, had a conservative majority which it lost in 1982. However, within the associations there usually exists a diversity of views, depending on the attitudes of individual local authorities, their relative strength in the political arena, and indeed, the standing and status of certain individuals – it is no single factor which decides to what level the LEAs will negotiate. However, even when a decision has been reached, the LEAs still need to consider the attitude of the government. The government, whilst not present at the negotiations, is the determining force. Whatever agreement is reached has to be accepted by the Secretary of State, and clearly, throughout the negotiations, government makes it pretty clear how far it is prepared to go. Sometimes, there is disagreement between local authorities and the government; more often, certainly in the last eight years, the local education authorities have found government restrictions on pay a convenient means of restricting pay settlements. In the 1960s and early 1970s, the Association of Education Committees (AEC), was lead by its powerful and dominant secretary – Sir William Alexander, who was nationally recognised as the spokesman for the local education authorities. His annual appearances at the Conference of the National Union of Teachers always produced a dramatic interlude: his blunt, colourful and aggressive style of oratory often annoyed the teachers; nevertheless, he was a powerful spokesman for the educational interests as such, and instrumental in achieving negotiated pay settlements. With the reform of local government in 1974, the Association of Education Committees was disbanded and Sir William disappeared from the scene.

The disappearance of the AEC marked a downgrading of the education service, which no longer has a national association of education committees. This has undoubtedly weakened the education lobbies in the localities, and there is no sign of a revival of the AEC. On the contrary, all the factors point to a continued struggle within town and county halls to reduce the influence of the education committees. The growth of powerful policy and resources committees within each local authority now stand between education committees and the full councils. The rise of chief executives or personnel managers to whom directors of education are sometimes subordinate, marks a further downgrading of the service. Such trends in local government are inevitably reflected in the Burnham Committee, and prominent LEA representatives who, in the past, made their reputations as education spokesmen, have been replaced by a different kind of person whose interest is finance rather than education.

Negotiations within the Burnham Committee are formal and one-dimensional. The only people who ever speak in the full committee are the leaders of the two panels, and occasionally the chairman. No one else says a word. The teachers' leader presents a claim after many hours of debate between the constituent associations. The local authorities then withdraw to argue amongst themselves; eventually they return and their leader replies to the claim, usually rejecting it and making a counter offer. The teachers then withdraw, argue amongst themselves, reach a conclusion, either by agreement or majority vote, and return to reply to the local education authorities, usually maintaining their claim. The local authorities listen, withdraw, and in due course respond, rejecting what the teachers have asked for. This goes on for several days, and may drag on for several months. Eventually, the only agreement which is recorded is the agreement to disagree and submit the whole issue to arbitration though even this eluded the committee in the last negotiations in April, 1982. All parties then prepare detailed and lengthy statements for the arbitration body, and have the right to appear before it. The arbitration body, having listened to both sides and studied the documentation, then makes a decision on levels of pay. This is communicated to the Secretary of State who, on behalf of the government, may or may not accept it. The Teachers' Remuneration Act enables the government to set aside any agreed settlement between teachers and employers, or any arbitration recommendation providing there is a majority in the House of Commons, and impose its own salary scales on the teachers. Furthermore, a 1981[7] amendment to the Act now requires both the teachers and their employers to agree to arbitration; previously, it was for the Chairman to decide whether or when negotiations had broken down. The latest sanctions imposed by the teachers in April, 1982 were not related to the size of their pay claim, but were mounted because the employers exercised this new power and refused to go to arbitration. This caused a storm of indignation among the teachers, resulting in almost unanimous support, in all professional associations, of sanctions involving withdrawal from lunch time supervising and from other voluntary activities. Appendix 2 gives details of the type of action mounted by the NUT. In the event, the teachers won the day; the employers agreed to arbitration after a serious rift between the labour controlled Association of Metropolitan Authorities, and the conservative controlled Association of County Councils. It is clear that the 1981 legislation, making arbitration dependent on the agreement of both parties to the negotiations has hindered, rather than helped, the whole process of salary negotiations; it is safe to assume that no action would have been initiated by the teachers had recourse to arbitration taken place on breakdown, as in previous circumstances.

The machinery for negotiating teachers' pay has been seriously criticised, and there is no doubt that some of the proceedings border on absurdity. It is certainly an absurd situation to bring together regularly, 60 or more busy teachers' and local education authorities' representatives, place them in separate rooms for long periods to argue amongst themselves, and finally, leave it to another body to make the final decision. The writer served on the Burnham Committee for four years, and found it a frustrating experience. No genuine negotiations took place, partly because each side knew that, whatever the outcome, the final decision would be made by the government; and partly because the procedures in the Committee did not lend themselves to talking round a table. Nor does the wrangling which goes on between the teachers' organisations do credit to the profession. Sometimes, the National Association of Schoolmasters and Women Teachers fails to participate and has been known to walk out. It is said that the only sensible people are the Welsh who go to the pub and wait until it is time to cast a vote. A reform of the Burnham machinery is urgently necessary to enable the two sides to attempt genuine negotiations, without feeling the heavy hand of the government throughout the proceedings, and yet not knowing just how much the government will, in the end, be prepared to pay out; furthermore, the Teachers' Remuneration Act makes it possible for the government to set aside any agreed pay settlement, which adds further frustration and uncertainty to the whole business.

However, it is one thing to be critical of the functioning of the Burnham Committee, but quite another to call for its abolition, for what is to take its place? The Civil Servants have done no better than the teachers through their negotiating machinery; the review bodies controlling the pay settlements for doctors and dentists have recently awarded these groups 6 per cent – 'in the light of economic conditions' – which is exactly the same amount which the arbitrators awarded the Scottish teachers in April, 1982 and the rest in June, 1982. What is needed is not only a reform of procedures, but a recognition that reasonably paid teachers are better teachers, that quality in the educational process is an investment in the future, that teachers do indeed 'produce' something worthwhile – in fact a change in the relationship between central government, local government and the teachers, based on the belief that harmony is better than controversy, and that the climate which exists during salary negotiations is itself a vital factor in achieving, or failing to achieve, agreement. Here, the first and major move must come from a Secretary of State with the conviction that the education service does matter, and with the strength of purpose, and indeed the personality, to put up the necessary fight in the Cabinet; the salary bill looks big, but is it really big? Here are the figures for the past three years, based on a teaching force of approximately 475,000:

	£ million
April 1979 –	2,424
April 1980 –	3,550
April 1981 –	3,812

The April 1982 salary bill amounted for £3,950 million for 455,000 teachers.[8] Assuming that seven lessons per day are given in 36,000 schools, the cost per lesson, using 200 teaching days, is about £75 per lesson; if we assume an average size class contains 30 pupils, the country spends just over £2 on each child in every lesson given – hardly big money! It all depends on the basis of calculation – but we have become so accustomed to being blinded by big figures, that the real cost, per child, is never mentioned!

Conditions of Service

The other great controversy relates to the inability of the Burnham Committee to discuss the teachers' conditions of service. The employers, the LEAs, are bitter about the fact that conditions of service cannot be discussed at the same time as salaries. They regard this as artificial, accuse the teachers of burying their heads in the sand, and point to the general pattern of negotiations between unions and employers, which always includes conditions of work, and in particular, the length of the working day. The teachers retort that Burnham was never designed to discuss conditions of service as well as salaries. It is highly unlikely that agreement would be reached on the complex issues relating to teachers' conditions of service which are the result of many conventions, informal agreements, and precedents, not the least of which is the teachers' willingness, stretching back over the years, to work voluntarily far beyond the time spent at school. Whilst Burnham cannot cope with pay, it is not likely to cope with anything else.

This however, is not to say that conditions of service, even if not discussed, fail to influence pay levels. In 1981, CLEA (Council of Local Education Authorities) pressed the teachers for new contracts on conditions of service, to be agreed before the 1981 pay negotiations were to be included. The gap between the two sides was considerable. The local authorities wanted teachers to agree to contracts which included 205 working days in school, a 37½ hour week, made up of 27½ hours class contact time, a minimum of 2½ hours for marking and preparation, and 7½ hours for other professional duties. The National Union of Teachers, suggested a 190 working year, five days set aside for in-service training, a 32½ hours week made up of 22 hours in the classroom, 5½ hours for preparation and marking, and five hours for other professional duties. The Union also pressed that the controversial lunch time duties should remain voluntary and the teachers' lunch hour breaks should be safeguarded; furthermore, the Union wanted class sizes to be part of any agreement, asked the LEAs to agree that no class should exceed 30 in any type of school, with admission classes in infants' schools to be 27, clearly defined limitations on the size of remedial teaching groups, and of classes having lessons in the practical subjects. The National Association of Schoolmasters and Union of Women Teachers boycotted the talks on conditions of service altogether. But just how hard, and how long, do teachers work?

As things stand, conditions of service are extremely flexible. Much is left to the individual school and particularly to the individual head-teachers to decide timetables, marking periods, supervision duties and the many variables which make up the teachers' day. Even more is left to the individual teacher to decide for himself how much work he does out of school; the time teachers spend on lesson preparations and marking, on extra curricular activities, on attending parent/teacher functions, and on the multitude of activities which go on in a school, beyond the task of teaching, is a matter for each individual teacher to decide for himself, and many teachers consider that the power to make this decision is the hallmark of being a professional.

However, there is growing up within the profession a powerful body of opinion, which is likely to gain strength in the next decade, which favours a contract which sets out more precisely what the teachers are supposed to do. The sacred cow of deciding for oneself, when set against the realities of the situation, looks less and less sacred. The fact is that the pressures on teachers are such that the vast majority of them undoubtedly work considerably longer than 37 hours a week. Research carried out by the National Foundation for Educational Research[9] suggests that teachers work at least 42 hours weekly, and many of them, particularly those in senior positions, work 60 to 70 hours, or even longer. The NFER study thoroughly researches the teachers' working day, extensively sampling class contact time, work done during lunch and break periods, at weekends, out of school hours and during holidays. No one has challenged the painstaking method which reveals, on the one hand, considerable variations throughout the country, and on the other, conclusions which most teachers will recognise immediately as applying to themselves.

> The evidence of our study — which has considered the teachers' total professional commitment and not just his class contact time and his school hours — suggests that the label '9 to 4' commonly attributed to the teaching job needs to be changed to 9 to 5.15; if the time taken for a midday meal is included, this becomes a few minues short of '9 to 6'.[10]

The analysis makes a useful distinction between 'C' time (teaching time) and 'S' time (teachers' overtime) including the result of careful observation and recording in all types of schools, reducing the multifarious activities of teachers to 55 categories, and examining professional work done on 200 schooldays, 75 weekends and during 150 holiday periods. Allowing for inevitable variations, the results show an average working week in term time of 41.3 hours, excluding 3.25 hours of weekend work, which consists largely of marking and lesson preparation, and considerable evening marking; during holidays, the study concluded that a typical teacher worked on half the holidays allotted during Christmas, Easter and Summer; and during half-term breaks, he worked on three or four of every five days allotted.

There is little doubt that pressures on teachers have increased consierably since the NFER study, and a similar investigation carried out today would yield longer hours and more days spent at work.

Lunch Time Duties

A major obstacle preventing real progress in conditions of service negotiations is the controversy concerning lunch time supervision. Here, there is a great difference in the way local education authorities and teachers interpret the existing agreement.[11] Teachers have always held that all lunch time supervision is purely voluntary, except for short periods at the beginning and end of morning and afternoon sessions, 10 to 15 minutes, when teachers are expected to be on the school premises and supervise pupils. The authorities retort that the head-teacher cannot divest himself of the responsibility for the safety and welfare of the pupils, and that he is therefore responsible throughout the lunch hour when pupils are on the premises, and by implication, needs some help to do his job. The teachers say that it is the job of local authorities in accordance with the agreement made, to provide ancillary supervision at the rate of at least one supervisor to 200 children. Where headteachers feel that such arrangements are inadequate, they should inform the authority that they can no longer accept responsibility unless supervision arrangements were strengthened.

What happens in practice? It is quite clear that teachers, other than heads, have succeeded in ensuring that their members, of whatever union, other than the Professional Association of Teachers, treat lunch time duties as purely voluntary, and headteacher members of all unions accept this situation as *de facto* if not always *de jure*. During the past two years, the NUT, NAS/UWT and AMMA have applied the powerful sanctions of requesting members to withdraw from voluntary supervision during the lunch hour during a dispute. Whilst many teachers dislike this kind of action, and point to the unfavourable publicity which some schools received when children were shut out from the school premises, creating, in some cases, disturbances and confrontation between teachers and pupils, the vast majority of teachers followed their union's lead, and showed that withdrawal from lunch duties was an effective weapon in using teacher power.

However, it is not only a question of supervising the school meals, but supervising the whole school. Many children are on the school premises, even if they do not take a school meal, others may bring sandwiches, others leave the school for a short time, spending at least half the lunch hours there. In thousands of schools up and down the country, extra curricular activities take place during the lunch hour. Thousands of lessons are given by teachers in a voluntary capacity, ranging from helping backward readers, to teaching 'S' level classes, providing foreign language conversation practice, additional examination preparation — all taught outside the timetable. The provision of school meals is therefore part of the functioning of the whole school during a vital period of the day. Not surprisingly, the local education authorities are extremely anxious to include in the teachers' conditions of service a clear understanding that for some of the time, teachers should be compelled to supervise during the lunch hour, so that the head is not left by himself, as is sometimes the case.

Other points of disagreement between the teachers and their employers relate to attendance at staff meetings, and particularly at parent/teacher interviews, usually held in the evenings. The notion that teachers can be asked to do 'reasonable duties' beyond school hours is capable of many interpretations, and there is no typical pattern of staff meetings throughout the country, except that they nearly all are held, by their very nature, out of school hours, and are thus treated as voluntary by teachers. The position is even more varied as far as parent/teacher interviews are concerned; a small school may not find it necessary to have more than one evening a year, as parents are in any case, in close contact with the teachers; a large comprehensive school can have 20 or 30 such consultative evenings; not only do teachers attend voluntarily, but — unbelievable to many other workers — they even have to pay their own expenses, as by no means all LEAs make provision for travelling expenses.

How should teachers react to the pressures brought on them by the local education authorities? What is likely to be the outcome of the present negotiations? It is at once obvious that a professional dimension is not at all incompatible with definite hours of work. Doctors are a case in point: surgery hours are limited, and doctors have a clear arrangement with each other in covering their patients' needs; health centres are organised on the principle that doctors are available during certain hours. Clearly there are circumstances, for example, emergencies, when doctors must, and do work well beyond stated hours, but the basic approach to their pay links conditions of service with salaries. Whilst such a link may not be in the interests of teachers, a more precise definition of their service conditions is certainly necessary.

There is no doubt that the pressures on teachers will increase as the cuts bite, and educational provision deteriorates. A clear limitation of hours would therefore work to the advantage of many thousands of overworked teachers, and could lead to the employment of many teachers who are available, but cannot get a job.

There is yet another problem crying out for a solution: the continuous class contact of primary teachers leads to immense pressures and not surprisingly, discontentment with their conditions as compared to secondary teachers. Primary teachers seldom experience a non-teaching period. This is even more true of infant teachers who, whilst having some help from welfare assistants, never leave a class during the whole of the day. It is an outrageous assumption that the only people who are entitled to non-contact time are secondary teachers, whereas those working with younger children are expected to have continuous contact throughout the day. It is part of an elitist tradition in education which needs challenging, and changing. Agreements on conditions of service should apply to all teachers irrespective of the type of schools in which they teach, recognising clearly the need to put aside time for duties other than teaching.

To argue for less contact time, and more closely defined conditions of service, is to argue on behalf of the vast majority of teachers, who do an extremely conscientious job, spending many hours at home and giving freely of their time after school hours. It is not to deny the existence of a small minority who have succeeded in arranging their professional life in such a way that they do as little as possible out of school, and indeed, sometimes as little as possible in school. In those staffrooms containing such teachers, there is both irritation and frustration when one teacher is seen to 'get away with it', whereas others are working hard and conscientiously. In most staffrooms the climate of opinion is such that few teachers, even those who may have lost their enthusiasm, get away with doing too little. However, there are the black sheep, and providing they give their lessons, heads are powerless to ask for more. They cannot order them to participate in extra curricular activities; nor can they control the amount of time spent in preparation, even if marking of written work can be monitored. Whilst a tighter contract would not eliminate the lazy teacher, it would force him to give a minimum commitment, make it more difficult to evade duties, and the majority of teachers would feel that justice has been done.

The other aspect which needs to be examined is the promotion of teachers, to be considered in the next chapter, and the relationship between getting more money for doing more work, and carrying greater responsibility. There is a very clear understanding in the vast majority of schools, that those who get paid most, beginning with the head, should do most. Heads of departments, teachers on Scale 3 posts and above, are expected by their colleagues, both to carry greater responsibility and to work longer hours. The justification for giving senior members of the profession somewhat less class contact time is simply that they could not do their job at all if they stood in front of a class all day. It is a recognition that what they have to do outside the classroom requires many hours, whether it is the organisation of a department in a secondary school, the commitment to pastoral work, requiring many hours of seeing parents, or making the school time-table, forcing many heads and deputies to work well into the summer holidays; all this needs time. A formula which clearly linked seniority to conditions of service, without being too rigid, would do much to create a clear understanding of what seniority entails, and is something which commends itself to many teachers.

Scottish Teachers

It is interesting, and relevant to our discussions, that north of the border, such problems have not only been recognised, but solved to a considerable extent. The Scottish teachers' conditions of service, usually referred to as 'the Contract' covers working hours, class contact time, class sizes, leave entitlements, in-service training, travelling allowances, grievance procedures, and is a model well worth looking at for English negotiators.[12] For secondary teachers the working week is laid down as 32½ hours, exclusive of lunch and other breaks, and including work done at home; this is based on a school week of some 27 hours which operates in most Scottish secondary schools. The exclusion of the lunch break removes any doubt and establishes that lunch time duties are voluntary. On the thorny issue of class contact time, which varies in Scotland as it does in England, according to type of school, school policy, and staffing, the contract states that there must be at least 200 minutes of non-contact time during each week of normal school hours, and that any infringement of that limit, caused by emergencies, by absence of colleagues, must be 'repaid' under a system agreed within the school. No significant problems have been experienced – the Scottish teachers know where they stand. In the matter of class size, the contract specifies a 'normal' maximum of 33 to 30 per class, with 20 in practical subjects, with a curious proviso that there may be an upper limit of 39 in class containing younger children, and 34 in others. This will seem too high for many English teachers, who feel that 30 is too many, but it should be noted that if the upper limit is used, the teacher concerned has the right to appeal to an adjudicating panel containing two teachers and two employers' representatives, with an appeals procedure to a national panel. Since 1976, only six cases have been heard by panels, and with falling rolls, it is likely that the problem of class size will feature less significantly in negotiations. Before the Scottish agreement was concluded, many teachers were worried that authorities would raise class sizes to the agreed maximum; the employers were worried that the agreement would lead to greater rigidity in school organisations. Neither fear was borne out by experience; the Scottish teachers have secured conditions of service which, by and large, satisfy them, and the employers have seen the advantages too.

What then, should be done to improve matters, both in the field of salaries and in conditions of service? First and foremost, there needs to be a clear recognition, both by employers and the teachers, that they share one common interest which is, or ought to be, greater than the sum total of all the differences: to protect and advance the interests of the nations' children. This obvious truth has been pushed aside, ignored, forgotten or conveniently brought up at intervals, but not really taken seriously. In an era which thrives on confrontation, the service desperately needs harmony rather than controversy. A successful school, a good family, thrives on harmony, and is destroyed by excessive controversy; those who are given responsibility, be they teachers or employers' representatives, ought to be chosen for their ability to reach agreement, and to be known for their genuine care and concern for children — or they have no business to be there. There is no simple recipe for bringing this about, but at least the criteria should be stated. A start can be made by the government, of whatever complexion, either stating clearly, from the outset, what it is prepared to find in the way of teachers' pay, which would at least have the merit of honesty, or leaving the two sides in a genuine, free, collective bargaining position. The two sides ought to agree on sensible procedures; Burnham could be reduced in size; different groups, composed of both teachers and employers, could talk about specific aspects of pay policy, so that people actually talk to one another, and hopefully, improve the climate in which negotiation takes place. Finally, conditions of service ought to be agreed at least to the extent they are in Scotland, to provide a base for future progress. Reason and enlightenment, other than dramatic posturings, are desperately needed. The same ingredients which make a good lesson, and a good teacher, are the requisites for reform.

Notes

1. 'Houghton and Clegg' — an analysis by John Hughes, Principal of Ruskin College, Oxford, and Director of the Trade Union Research Unit — see *Times Educational Supplement*, 2 May 1980.

2. Standing Commission on Pay Comparability (Clegg Report) Report No. 7, Cmnd 7880 (HMSO, London, April, 1980). Chapter three, 'Evidence', p. 8.

3. *Falling Rolls in Secondary Schools* by Briault and Francis Smith – Part 1 (NFER, London, April, 1980).

4. 'Falling Rolls and the Burnham Alternatives' – W.F. Dennison, *Secondary Education Journal*, NUT, London, March, 1980. 'Decline and Fall: How to Cope' – Martin Pick – *Education Guardian*, 29 April 1980. 'Salary Policy for the Burnham Report, 1982–3. Statement by Executive to Annual Conference', 1981 (NUT). 'The Reform of the Burnham Structure' – NUT Discussions Document, NUT, London. January, 1981.

5. 'Report of Committee of Inquiry into Pay of non-University teachers', Houghton Report (HMSO, London, 1974) and Clegg Report (HMSO, London, 1980).

6. Composition of Burnham Committee:

Teachers' Panel		Management Panel	
NUT	16	Association of County Councils	14
NAS/UWT	7	Association of Metropolitan Authorities	10
AMMA	4	Welsh Joint Education Committee	2
NAHT	2	Department of Education and Science	2
SHA	1		
PAT	1		
NAFTHE	1		

Leaders of the two sides act as joint honorary secretaries.

7. Remuneration of Teachers Act – Mr Carlisle's (the then Secretary of State for Education and Science) reply to questions asked in the House of Commons by Mr M. Thornton, MP for Garston, 30 June 1981.

8. See Teachers Pay Factsheets, NUT, Hamilton House, London, July, 1982.

9. *The Teacher's Day* by S. Hilsum and B.S. Cane, National Foundation for Educational Research in England and Wales. London, 1971.

10. Ibid., p. 57.

11. 'Conditions of Tenure of Teachers': Recommendations of Joint Conference of Association of Education Committees, Association of Municipal Corporations, County Council Associations, and Welsh Joint Committee, NUT, Joint committee of Four Secondary Associations. NAHT, NAS (issued 1946, revised 1950, 1958, 1968 and 1972).

12. See 'Scottish Teachers Conditions of Service – The Contract'; Robert Beattie, *Secondary Educational Journal*, NUT, London. March, 1981.

Table 4.4: Salary Scales for Teachers (Old Scales: Until March 1982; New Scales: From 1 April 1982)

Point	Scale 1 Old £	Scale 1 New £	Scale 2 Old £	Scale 2 New £	Qualified Teachers Scale 2(S) Old £	Scale 2(S) New £	Scale 3 Old £	Scale 3 New £	Scale 3 (S) Old £	Scale 3 (S) New £	Scale 4 Old £	Scale 4 New £	Senior Teacher Old £	Senior Teacher New £	Point
0	4653	4932	5346	5667	5964	6321	6612	7008	7317	7755	7869	8340	8478	8988	0
1	4869	5160	5547	5880	6180	6552	6843	7254	7596	8052	8208	8700	8796	9324	1
2	5028	5331	5754	6099	6396	6780	7077	7503	7869	8340	8478	8988	9117	9663	2
3	5190	5502	5964	6321	6612	7008	7317	7755	8208	8700	8796	9324	9432	9999	3
4	5346	5667	6180	6552	6843	7254	7596	8052	8478	8988	9117	9663	9753	10338	4
5	5547	5880	6396	6780	7077	7503	7869	8340	8796	9324	9432	9999	10203	10815	5
6	5754	6099	6612	7008	7317	7755	8208	8700	9117	9663	9753	10338	10572	11205	6
7	5964	6321	6843	7254	7596	8052	8478	8988	9432	9999	10203	10815	11082	11748	7
8	6180	6552	7077	7503	7869	8340	8796	9324	9753	10338	10572	11205	11454	12141	8
9	6396	6780	7317	7755	8208	8700	9117	9663	10203	10815					9
10	6612	7008	7596	8052	8478	8988	9432	9999							10
11	6843	7254	7869	8340	8796	9324									11

Table 4.4: Continued

Group	Head Teachers Minimum Old £	New £	Maximum Old £	New £
1	8184	8676	9111	9657
2	8541	9054	9471	10038
3	8940	9477	9864	10455
4	9501	10071	10590	11226
5	10296	10914	11388	12072
6	11022	11682	12129	12858
7	11703	12405	12810	13578
8	12540	13293	13650	14469
9	13506	14316	14631	15510
10	14385	15249	15513	16443
11	15525	16458	16680	17682
12	16623	17619	17706	18768
13	17514	18564	18603	19719
14	18522	19632	19617	20793

Group	Special School Heads Minimum Old £	New £	Maximum Old £	New £
3(S)	9708	10290	10620	11256
4(S)	10287	10905	11358	12039
5(S)	11451	12138	12537	13290
6(S)	11835	12546	12924	13698
7(S)	12687	13449	13779	14607
8(S)	13293	14091	14397	15261
9(S)	13881	14715	15033	15936

Group	Deputy Head Teachers Minimum Old £	New £	Maximum Old £	New £
Below 4	5820	6168	8337	8838
4	6882	7296	8961	9498
5	7701	8163	9594	10170
6	8784	9312	9846	10437
7	9279	9837	10368	10989
8	9753	10338	10842	11493
9	10293	10911	11421	12105
10	10977	11637	12090	12816
11	11541	12234	12648	13407
12	12195	12927	13311	14109
13	12567	13320	13689	14511
14	13140	13929	14271	15126

Table 4.4: Continued

| Group | Special School Deputy Heads | | | |
| | Minimum | | Maximum | |
	Old £	New £	Old £	New £
3(S)	6741	7146	9186	9738
4(S)	7815	8283	9642	10221
5(S)	9303	9861	10362	10983
6(S)	9630	10209	10689	11331
7(S)	9972	10569	11025	11688
8(S)	10296	10914	11355	12036
9(S)	10953	11610	12021	12741

Source: Details supplied by NUT Salaries Department, Hamilton House, London, June 1982.

APPENDIX II

NEWS　　MARCH
NUT PAY SPECIAL

A call to every member

Immediately after the breakdown in Burnham on 3 March the NUT Executive was summoned to meet on 5 March. In order to secure the agreement by the Management Panel for the submission of the pay dispute to arbitration the Executive decided:-

(1) From Thursday, 11 March 1982 and until further notice members are called upon to:-
(a) refuse to supervise the taking of school meals;
(b) refuse to provide any oversight of pupils during the mid-day break;
(c) withdraw from the organisation of or assistance with all other voluntary activities during the mid-day break;
(d) refuse to undertake any administrative task connected with the school meals service

ALL MEMBERS ARE ADVISED TO LEAVE THE SCHOOL PREMISES DURING THE SCHOOL MEAL BREAK.

(2) Over the same period members are called upon to refuse to attend or participate in any voluntary activity connected with the administration of school, including parents' evenings and staff meetings which take place after school hours.

One objective of the action is to persuade your Education Authority to make a public declaration of its support for the stand taken by the Teachers' Panel and to achieve the support of political parties at local level. WHERE SATISFACTORY ASSURANCES ARE GIVEN BY YOUR LEA THE EXECUTIVE HAS INDICATED ITS WILLINGNESS TO SUSPEND THE SANCTION IN YOUR AREA. Your response to this action is of vital importance in this campaign in order to achieve the objective as early as possible.

In addition the Executive agreed to convene a meeting at the earliest possible date with the NAS/UWT to seek to co-ordinate action in this campaign. Further the Executive will seek to arrange a subsequent meeting of all of the major teacher organisations.

UNITED WE MUST STAND

In Burnham, all teachers' organisations agreed in rejecting the Management Panel's insulting offer of 3.4% and in deploring the refusal of the Management Panel to go to arbitration after it had held out no prospect of any improvement on the 3.4% offer.

All teachers' organisations agreed that they were not prepared for Burnham to adjourn to 2 April, the date proposed by the Management "to give both sides time to reflect on their respective situations".

The Teachers' Panel was ready to meet the Management Panel at any time provided there was the prospect of an improved offer and serious negotiations. What it was not prepared to do was attend another meeting of Burnham like the one on 3 March when no progress whatever was made.

The Teachers' Panel rejected the Management's contention that the Local Authorities are not able to pay more than 3.4%. Fred Jarvis, Leader of

the Teacher' Panel and General Secretary of the NUT, declared in Burnham that information reaching him showed clearly that many Local Authorities were setting aside substantially more than 3.4% for teachers' pay in their 1982/83 estimates. He said that if the Local Authorities were to maintain their self-respect they had to show they had a mind and will of their own and were not acting simply as agents of Government.

It is now essential that the unity shown in the Teachers' Panel is maintained in the weeks ahead and that all members of all organisations take action to increase the pressure on the Government and the Local Authorities.

5 PROMOTION

There is probably no topic of staffroom conversation which causes more concern, raises more hopes, and sees more hopes dashed, than that of promotion. Most teachers, at some stage in their careers, want it — whether it is a move up the ladder to the next scale, or whether the goal is a headship. What are the chances of obtaining promotion at all for teachers in the next decade? What is the likelihood of becoming a head of department, a deputy or a head — or simply to get away from the lowest salary scale? What factors affect promotion, who and what determines ones' chances? How does it all work and how should it work? What are the main barriers to promotion and how can they be overcome?

For some 70 years following the introduction of public education, the notion of promotion simply meant getting a headship. Until World War II, you were either a head teacher or a class teacher; deputy heads were appointed in grammar, later in secondary schools and eventually in the larger primary schools, and a woman, usually in charge of girls, was known as the 'Senior Mistress'. But class teachers accepted that they all did broadly the same job and should therefore draw roughly the same pay; salary increments based on length of service were accepted as the only way of earning more, the only justification for paying one teacher more than another.

The post-war era brought radical changes; the increasing complexity of schools, demands from within the profession for a clearly recognisable careers structure, and the employers' readiness to pay more to some teachers, led to the system of differentiated salary scales described in the previous chapter. It has never remained unchallenged; throughout the 1950s and early 1960s, the cry, at most teachers' conferences, was for a decent basic scale for everybody, and resistance to differential payments. The main battle between the NUT Executive and its membership, at every conference from the mid-1950s to the mid-1960s was on the basic scale. Eventually, the advocates of the basic scale faded away, to be replaced by new leaders wanting a fair deal for every teacher, linking promotion to different salary scales, and thus enabling every teacher to see clearly the existence of a promotion ladder; you start at Scale 1, move to Scales 2 and 3, and if you are lucky, with good qualifications and happen to teach in a secondary

78

school, to Scale 4. For the few, there is promotion to a Senior Teachers grade (again only available in secondary schools) and eventually to a deputy headship and headship, the rewards depending on the size of school.

Table 5.1 shows the distribution of teachers between the different salary scales.

Table 5.1: Percentage of Teachers on Different Salary Scales

Scale 1	31.5%
Scale 2	32.3%
Scale 3	14.9%
Scale 4	6.3%
Senior Teachers' Scale	1.4%
Heads and Deputy Heads	13.6%

Source: Figures supplied by NUT Salaries Department, April 1982.

What determines moves up the ladder? Does promotion inevitably mean a change of school? What are the chances of internal promotion?

The chances, at any time, in any type of school, are determined by the schools' unit total, which in turn determines the point score, which is then translated into a number of posts; it is essential to understand how the system works, and which factors make for or against the availability of above Scale 1 posts in any school on sole numerical criteria, before other factors are considered, for if the above scale posts are not there, nobody can have them.

Points Scores and Unit Totals

The Burnham Report[1] provides an age weighting for each pupil as follows:

Age

Under 14 years —	each pupil counts as 2 units
14-15	each pupil counts as 3 units
15-16	each pupil counts as 4 units
16-17	each pupil counts as 6 units
Over 17	each pupil counts as 8 units

By multiplying the age weighting by the number of pupils on roll, the 'unit total' is arrived at. The unit total for the smallest school in existence is less than 100; for a two-form entry primary school with 240 pupils on roll, covering age groups from seven to eleven, it is 480; for a large comprehensive with say, 1500, and a Sixth Form of over 200, it is between 5,000 and 7,000 units. The total number of unit totals determines the group of the school, which in turn determines the salary of the head and the deputy head; for the class teacher, it is the 'point score range' that makes or mars promotion chances; this is shown in the second column in the table below:

Table 5.2: Unit Totals, Point Score Ranges and School Groups

Unit Total or Review Average	Schools, other than Special Schools		
	Points Score range	Highest Scale for Teachers below Deputy Head Teacher	Group of School for Head and Deputy Head Teacher purposes
(1)	(2)	(3)	(4)
up to 100	0–1	2	1
101–200	0–1	2	2
201–300	0–2	2	3
301–400	1–3	2	4
401–500	2–6		
501–600	3–8	3	5
601–700	5–11		
701–800	7–13		
801–900	9–15	3	6
901–1000	10–17		
1001–1100	11–21		
1101–1200	13–23	3	7
1201–1300	14–26		
1301–1400	15–28		
1401–1600	17–33	4	8
1601–1800	21–37		
1801–2000	25–40		
2001–2200	30–44	4	9
2201–2400	35–49		
2401–2700	41–55		
2701–3000	47–60	4a	10
3001–3300	52–65		
3301–3700	57–74		
3701–4100	62–79	4a	11
4101–4600	68–83		
4601–5100	75–90		
5101–5600	81–96	4a	12
5601–6000	88–103		
6001–6100	88–103		
6101–6600	94–109	4a	13
6601–7100	101–116		
7101–7600	108–123		
Over 7600	Proportionately	4a	14

Note: a. Including Senior Teachers.
Source: Burnham Report, HMSO, Appendix II, p. 25, 1978.

The actual points score for each school is prescribed by the Local Education Authority, and in the majority of cases, lies at the midpoint: thus, a group 5 school with a unit total between 500 and 700, and a points score range of 3 to 11, will probably be given 7 points; in a generous authority, the maximum number of 11 points may be made available; in a mean authority – and there are some – only the minimum of 3 points is made available to the school.

Once the points score for a school is settled, the number of actual posts on the different scales can be determined; each teacher on Scale 2 counts as 1 point, on Scale 3, 2 points, on Scale 4 (and on the Senior Teachers' scale) 3 points: in our example, 7 points are available. The school could establish 7 posts at Scale 2, or 3 posts at Scale 3 and one at Scale 2. In a large comprehensive school with a score of say, 75 points, it is possible to have say, 10 posts at Scale 4 (30 points) 15 posts at Scale 3 (30 points) and 15 posts at Scale 2 (15 points); other variations are possible; LEAs, in such schools, also lay down the number of Senior Teachers' posts (maximum 4); finally, the LEAs may specify the number of teachers who may be on a deputy heads' scale, subject to a maximum of three.

Each school is reviewed every three years, for the purpose of checking its unit total, establishing the points score range and the number of posts available above Scale 1. This procedure is known as the 'triennial review' and the 'review average' is the unit total averages calculated over the three years period; however the Burnham Report makes special provision for newly opened and reorganised schools.

A number of factors are at once obvious: first, the age range and number of pupils clearly determine promotion chances in any given school at any given time; because of the operation of the points system and the age weighting such promotion chances are generally, though not invariably, better in secondary than in primary schools; second, the generosity or meanness of the local education authority (or, in some cases, the relative strength or weakness of the head and the governors in getting the LEA to grant points beyond the usual point score) must have an influence; LEAs have considerable discretion in these matters, and are in a position to establish points even if a school is already on its maximum.

Finally, teachers, once they hold an above Scale 1 post, are protected, i.e. they cannot lose their promoted post, even if the unit total of their school drops. Here, the numbers of pupils are of immense importance: At a time of falling rolls, promotion chances are clearly better in those areas where school rolls fall only slowly; as there is already evidence that primary rolls will actually increase in the late 1980s, teachers able to move freely should always look at such trends; conversely, areas in which rolls fall rapidly must, by the very nature of the mechanism, offer fewer and fewer promotion chances. Although a teachers' promoted post is protected whilst he or she remains on the staff of a school, the post lapses once the teacher leaves if the score is no longer high enough to warrant its retention.

Primary teachers have a long standing grievance at what many of them consider to be the unjust operation of a system which favours secondary schools. Surely, they say, a child is a child, and there is certainly a good case to be made for the infant teacher providing highly skilled attention for the diverse needs of an admission class of 30, to rank equal with the Oxbridge graduate teaching 'A' levels to a small group of clever sixth formers; although some adjustments have been made to narrow the gap — a decade ago, the under fourteens counted only 1 point, and the over seventeens scored 10 — the pyramidical structure of our educational system is still powerfully reflected in the careers structure for teachers.

Promoted Posts above Scale 1

But the number of points and posts available in a school at a given time, is of course, only part of the story. Who gets promoted, and who doesn't, and why? How much luck is there in the system? What are the obstacles? Is there discrimination, against whom and on what grounds?

There are no easy answers to such questions, but a number of studies[3] have been undertaken which throw some light on what happens. First, what do the majority of teachers want? Table 5.3 sets out teachers' aspirations as seen over a ten year period.

Table 5.3: Teachers' Aspirations and Expectations — All Teachers (Primary Plus Secondary) Given as a Percentage of 5,970 Teachers

Activity	Aspiration		Expectation	
	Rank	per cent	Rank	per cent
Teaching in schools	1	58.8	1	67.0
Retirement	2	10.1	2	13.3
Lecturer	3	9.3	4	4.5
Don't know	4	7.8	3	7.9
Related educational work	4	5.4	6	1.9
Administration	6	4.9	7	1.4
Non-educational/emigrate	7	3.7	5	4.0

Source: S. Hilsum and K.B. Start, (1974).

It will be seen that nearly 59 per cent want, and 67 per cent expect, to remain in school, the difference (8 per cent) presumably wanting to be elsewhere; the number of those looking forward to early retirement will almost certainly have increased since the NFER survey, and judging by the number of applications for early retirements handled by those local education authorities which have early retirement schemes with full, or reasonably generous enhancement of pensions, the figure is likely to be near 25 per cent, one in every four teachers. This of course, is not unrelated to the increasing stress[4] acknowledged to be part of a teacher's occupational hazard in the 1980s. Therefore, such trends undoubtedly enhance promotion chances for the young teacher, even in the present difficult times. Furthermore, the NFER survey says that aspirations for head and deputy head teachers posts are not 'alarmingly oversubscribed'; in secondary schools 11.8 per cent of teachers aspire to a headship, 6.9 per cent get it, and 5 per cent heads' posts are available; for deputies, the figures are 10.8 aspirants, 8.8 per cent expectations, 6.0 available. But for Scale 3 and 4 posts, the ratio of expectancy against available points is .90, whilst at Scale 2 it is only .20. Thus, there are many more secondary teachers looking forward to Scale 3 and Scale 4 posts, rather then being contented to stay on Scale 2; but by no means overlarge numbers are aspiring to be heads and deputy heads. The saying that there is 'plenty of room at the top' may be something of an overstatement but on the basis of numbers alone, even allowing for an accelerating rate of school closures, deputy headships and headships are still within the reach of many secondary teachers, who should certainly not be deterred from applying on the sole grounds that there are hundreds of applicants; this if often hearsay rather than fact.

Among primary teachers, the position is somewhat different. Some 62 per cent wanted to remain in teaching, and 40 per cent aspired to headships (25.7 per cent) or to deputy headships (14.3 per cent); 7 per cent wanted no responsibility, and were content to remain on Scale 1; but the level of expectation for a headship was 20.5 per cent against a 16 per cent availability; in the case of deputy headships 14.3 per cent had hopes against an availability of 10 per cent – not an impossible gap here. For Scale 2 and 3 posts in primary schools, the figures are surprising: only 16 per cent had hopes of promotion, but some 18 per cent, at the time of the survey, were satisfied. But the survey also noted that the youngest teachers, in the under 30 age group in primary schools, appeared 'unduly pessimistic' about getting a headship in ten years' time, but over optimistic about getting a post on Scale 2 or 3. Secondary teachers under 30 had considerable ambitions for higher posts in their own schools, which were not unrealistic; but only 1 per cent expected to get headships, and 4 per cent hoped for deputy headships.[5]

The figures underlying the NFER survey date back eight years, and it is likely that many of the teachers responding were not yet fully aware of the dramatic impact of falling rolls on schools, of the severity, and indeed the viciousness of the cuts in educational expenditure, and of the consequent lessening of mobility in the profession — many teachers, these days, sit tight and are undoubtedly glad to have a job. However, even allowing for these factors, promotion prospects are anything but hopeless, and indeed, even in these hard times, some teachers, somewhere, are promoted every day. It is pertinent, there-fore, to look at possible obstacles to promotion other than the simple, and supposed, non-availability of higher paid posts.

Here, the NUT's recent survey *A Fair Way Forward* yields rich and recent information. Initiated in response to a Conference resolution passed in 1979,[6] it reflected the deep disquiet felt by teachers both at the procedures and the anomalies inherent in the promotion stakes. The National Executive was instructed to undertake a thorough investi-gation of appointments and promotion procedures and to make recom-mendations. In the event, the investigation took two years to complete and provides the most up to date information on the issue. Local education authorities were approached and 63 per cent responded to a questionnaire covering every aspect of promotion — advertising policies, job descriptions, content and processing of applications; composition and functioning of interviewing bodies, and policies on restricted com-petition for posts. The union's divisions in 25 areas also replied; both sets of replies were analysed, circularised to the union's 580 constitu-tional associations for comment, yielding vast information both on local procedures and many individual case histories. Whilst complete accuracy cannot be guaranteed in each case, the picture that emerged showed what was happening, what teachers felt and how they fared in the promotion race.

Confidential Reports

The immediate and most striking findings related to the highly unsatis-factory nature as to the use and misuse of confidential reports. Teachers have always disliked the practice of local authorities, or headteachers acting on their behalf, seeking reports in confidence, either in writing or on the telephone; the NUT's professional conduct code has for many years, expressly declared the making of such reports as unprofessional:

> the following is a list of actions declared to be unprofessional . . . for any teacher to make a report on the work or conduct of another teacher without at the time acquainting the teacher concerned with the nature of it, if it be a verbal report, or without showing it, if it be written, and allowing the teacher concerned to take a copy of it.[7]

However, until the publication of the survey it was accepted that if a teacher asked the head of a school, or any other teacher, to act as a referee, confidentiality was allowed. However, the recommendation accepted by the 1982 Conference firmly and specifically stated that the union was opposed to all forms of confidentiality, without exception, and particularly stated that reports should be neither sought not given on the telephone. Furthermore, it was recommended that the union's professional conduct code should form the basis of a national agreement applicable to all employing authorities and to all teachers.

Such a reform is long overdue. There is no doubt that the existence of a system of confidential reports not only makes possible biased and unfair reporting, but is not really useful. A local authority wishing to retain an existing teacher, or head teacher, responding to the request of another employer, may write a good report; but the LEA's senior inspector – if he writes the report – may sound just that note of reservation which makes the difference as to whether one gets on the short list or not. A headteacher wishing to encourage a teacher to move elsewhere, or simply wanting to get rid of him could write a report which is markedly better than the teachers' professional competence warrants. Such things are the exception in some areas, but are known to exist in others. The fact is that abuses do happen; everyone involved knows this, even though it is difficult, and usually impossible, to prove it. There is no case for continuing such a system, which must, by its very nature, lead to mistrust, suspicion, and to bad professional relations, without any obvious advantages. Teachers must be, and usually are, willing to discuss their professional difficulties with one another; often they are not of the individual teacher's making, nor can they always be laid at the door of a particular head. A school in a difficult area, or one starved of resources, or badly organised, must make it more difficult for teachers to do their job, and there is no shortage of schools starved of resources in the 1980s. Nor is the issue of confidential reports entirely a matter between headteachers and class teachers; heads themselves, if they wish to move, are subject to the confidential reports procedure: the quality of their professional leadership, the evaluation of their role, are the subject of comment by education officers, and sometimes the chairman of governors of education committees, or of the local inspector; heads, like class teachers, have neither access nor redress; indeed, they may never know just what is said about them, or who said it.

It is no excuse to state that the majority of education officers or inspectors are people of high professional integrity and write unbiased reports. This is not always so; we live in turbulent, difficult times, and if often falls to heads of schools to defend the interests of their school, even if this means being critical of the local education authority which employs them, and sometimes, challenging the decision of the officers of the authority, who are themselves subject to increasingly powerful direction from the controlling politicians. An 'awkward' head might be 'encouraged' to move on, by making him appear better than he is; a good head might be retained even if he or she wishes to move, because it suits the circumstances of a particular case. A headteacher, acting in the best interest of his school, will, these days, often find himself in a position of wanting to recruit a teacher of a particular subject, owing to curriculum changes; another teacher blocks the way, and because of staffing constraints, cannot or sometimes will not, move. There is only one way to deal with such matters — abolish confidential reports altogether, without exception, without reservation.

There are additional reasons why this should be done. The tolerance level of our society is lower than it has been in the recent past; extremists on either side of the political spectrum are not only in evidence, but sometimes in control. The NUT's working party on Appointments and Promotions found widespread anxiety among teachers that both their professional views and in particular, their union activity, hampered their progress. There were reports stating that particular views favouring mixed ability teaching cost a candidate promotion in a situation where the chairman of the governors did not believe in it, even though the headteacher operated it. There were also reports where advocacy of setting and a cautious approach to mixed ability teaching found no favour at interview and the job went to another. Even more disturbing were reports of questions relating to the candidate's domestic circumstances, marital status, plans for having children, and even political and religious matters (though the last, do, of course have a place in appointments to denominational schools). The criteria for promotion should be professional competence and relevant experience, not subjective evaluation of teachers' personal affairs.

Women Teachers and Discrimination

There is a persistent feeling among women teachers that they face considerable discrimination not only when applying for appointments as such, but particularly when going for promotion. Discrimination against women was, of course, very real in the first half of this century, and it was not until the achievement of equal pay for women teachers that a real inroad was made into the more flagrant discriminatory practices, such as refusing appointments to women because they were married. But what is the position today, at a time when legislation has been specifically enacted to prevent such discrimination? Are the fears of women that their chances of obtaining professional advancement are less than those of men teachers still justified?

The thoroughly documented investigation by the NFER[8] says surprisingly little about this issue, and seems to have missed, or misjudged, matters of continuous concern to women teachers. There is a peculiar distinction between 'normal' and 're-entrant' teachers, that is those who return to teaching after bringing up a family. The latter are said, proportionately, to be more willing to stay unpromoted than the 'normal' women. We have to turn to the NUT's detailed investigation on 'Promotion and the Woman Teacher'[9] to get at some facts: A random sample of 2,829 women teachers answered a detailed questionnaire with honesty and wry humour; their collective view about themselves coincides with that of an early NUT woman President, Miss E. Conroy, speaking in 1918:

> If the woman is to fulfil her proper place in the educational system, it will be necessary for her to be acknowledged, when fully trained and qualified, as the equal of her male colleague, with the same opportunities for development and promotion as he enjoys . . . Many women begin the work of teaching with high hopes of usefulness in life, and are endowed with an inborn love of the work . . . but it is difficult for a woman to keep these ideals when she realises that she is relegated to the lower rungs of the educational ladder, however capable she may be . . . The ideal teacher is rare and I claim that such a person is as likely to be discovered among women in quite

as great a proportion as among men.

The findings of the report support the contention that women do not, generally, get a square deal: they represent 59 per cent of the profession, but hold only 38 per cent of the headships. 78 per cent of the women, as against 49 per cent of the men, are on the lowest two salary scales. Some 10 per cent of all men, but only 4 per cent of all women teachers, are heads; women teachers represent 77 per cent of the teaching force in primary schools, but hold only 43 per cent of the headships. Finally, only 28 per cent of those answering the survey had small children. However, the success rate for internal promotion was nearly twice as high as with external applications. Allowing for the lower mobility of women teachers, this indicates that once their worth is known – within their own schools – it is often recognised.

However, whilst the statistics tell a pretty conclusive story, it is less easy to pinpoint individual cases of discrmination. It is known from the type of questions often asked at interviews, particularly those relating to the husband's occupation and ages of children, that these factors must weigh with many interviewing panels. The provisions allowing women to return after maternity leave are not yet widely seen as good. Teachers with a break in service are not always welcome to all appointing authorities. However, women teachers can take heart from the fact that the climate is changing; the very existence of the Equal Opportunities Commission, the greater involvement of women as governors and on appointing bodies, and the growth of more enlightened attitudes on the part of heads and education officers are making an impact – in the writer's present school, two women and two men gained senior posts, including headships in the last two years; in his previous school, the ratio was one to six. The myth that women have a low promotion orientation is becoming less and less accepted, and the teachers' campaign for non-discriminatory treatment, with insistence that the professional criteria should determine promotions is likely to gain more and more ground in the next few years.

Teachers' promotions are vitally affected by the methods used in processing applications, and particularly by the composition of interviewing bodies. Such factors are difficult to measure: the NUT survey found widely differing practices in shortlisting applicants; whilst in 88 per cent of the responding local authorities the head was involved, either alone, or with education officials, there was at least one authority where the chairman and vice-chairman of the education committee were involved even in the appointment of Scale 1 teachers.

Headships

Applicants for headships usually passed through a 'sieve'; criteria relating to minimum and maximum age, relevant experiences and qualifications were worked out and senior education officials sifted the applications before the chief education officers, or one of his senior assistants, looked at the sifted applications and produced a 'long short list', which then became the final short list after the deliberations of an appointing committee of school governors, or at least the chairman, and/or senior councillors serving on education committees. The selection of heads must, by its very nature, be a complicated and risky task; even a good deputy does not necessarily make a good head. The skills required of a successful head are multi-dimensional – organising ability, good communicative powers, tact and firmness in the management of people, a thorough understanding of the educational practice and a good grasp of educational ideas; having an air of authority without being an authoritarian; understanding the need for acceptability by pupils, staff and parents; being capable of a positive approach to public relations; managing resources; being able to delegate, and monitor adequately what is happening inside the school; above all, having the necessary physical and psychological stamina to do an increasingly difficult and complex job – all such qualities do not abound in every person appointed. But perhaps the greatest deficiency in the appointment of heads is that they are simply not trained for the job – they are in the classroom one day, and in the head's study the next, with deputies in the largest comprehensive being the only group with real managerial experiences before being promoted. Although some in-service courses attempt to deal with such gaps, these are often too short, and sometimes not really designed, to make a real impact. What is needed, without any doubt, is deliberate training for heads, and preferably, also for deputies, in a special institution, preferably a Staff College. The need is for the aspirants to have the opportunity, on a full-time basis, to leave their own schools for a time, see what goes on elsewhere, learn in detail the main components of a head's day-to-day work, think, read and talk to other people, and above all, engage in rigorous self-evaluation, as well as being evaluated by the staff of such a college, before taking the plunge. The establishment of such a college[11] is long overdue: it is absurd that in-service training should cover every facet of the curriculum, every detail of school organisation ranging from the pastoral system to the introduction of computer methodology, and yet leave out the training of those who have the ultimate responsibility, or at best, deal with it in a piecemeal, superficial fashion. A blueprint for such a college is not difficult to design:

the courses should consist of dealing with those issues which face heads every day without delving too deeply into educational philsophy; there should be an opportunity for 'on the spot' training by enabling candidates to work alongside, during the course, successful heads, or even, occasionally, alongside unsuccessful ones. The staff of such a college should be drawn largely from those who are doing, or have done, the job successfully themselves, though an input from education officers, inspectors, and parents, employers and other interest groups should be part of the staple diet. Practising teachers, non-heads, who have to work with the heads, also need to be involved, preferably on a basis of seconding them, for a period of time, from their present appointments. Just as the medical or legal profession trains its own senior post holders, so the teaching profession needs a structured, well designed course, which makes the appointment of heads less of a risk, or less dependent on the vagaries of the present system.

The involvement of teacher governors of individual schools, and teacher representatives on education committees in the selection process for appointing heads is another much needed reform. The teachers are in day-to-day contact with children, with parents, and with other teachers, an advantage which no lay members, or education officers can claim. This is not to say that in a democratic society, the professionals should have the last word. What is being argued is the need for far greater involvement of the professional, the need to resist the tide of lay opinions which, in more and more cases has overridden the advice of chief education officers since the mentality of the Baines report has downgraded the education service with its insistence on 'corporate responsibility' with no corporate bottom to be kicked when wrong appointments are made.

The NUT's *A Fair Way Forward* recommended strongly that selection of long and short lists should never be the work of only one person; that, at school level, it should be the responsibility of the appropriate professionals, with the school itself playing the major part. This reflects a practice which has grown particularly since the advent of comprehensive schools, whose heads of departments inevitably and rightly, are consulted by heads, see the candidates and frequently sit alongside LEA advisers and governors on appointment committees. It may be argued that this means a lessening of democratic control. But what criteria should be followed in making senior appointments? Is the inevitably superficial judgment of elected representatives, seeing candidates for an inevitably short period, often not likely to exceed half an hour, with several candidates to be seen within a tightly drawn interviewing schedule, the best way to ensure that the community is well served? Has not the head of the school, and the head of the department and other teachers alongside whom the person appointed must work, and who knows precisely what is needed, a greater incentive to make an appointment on grounds of purely professional competence? Anecdotes of questions being asked at interview by councillors which have neither relevance nor understanding abound — they are not all exaggerated: 'I know, Mr X, you have a good honours degree, but have you passed your matriculation?' is not a sick joke, but based on countless experiences of countless teachers attending countless interviews. The NUT survey found that 90 per cent of the responding local authorities did not issue guidelines for use by interviewing panels, and LEAs deserve credit for openly admitting this to be the case. Whilst one third of the respondents claimed to have wide criteria for the evaluation of candidates, few gave any indication of what those were. What is clear is that the power of patronage, and in particular, political patronage, is firmly in the hands of politicians; anyone who has been a teacher representative, or been involved in senior appointments knows the resistance to professional advisers, and insistence on the person 'we want' is a real feature of the appointing process. Sometimes it works, sometimes it doesn't. The risk is too great to be taken. What is needed is the evolution of specific criteria related clearly to a carefully drafted specification, with appropriate weighting to be given to each criterion.

But a lessening of discrimination, improving the machinery and the techniques for making promoted appointments are not, by themselves, enough. The teaching profession must help itself to become more professional, and must be helped in doing this by the local authorities. Teachers themselves are clearly aware of the criteria which ought to be applied; the NFER listed the following factors, that teachers believed should favour promotion, in order of their size across the sample of both primary and secondary teachers, 13 factors emerging as top from a possible list of 31:

1. Flexibility in teaching methods
2. Familiarity with new ideas
3. Ability to control pupils
4. Concern for pupil welfare
5. Variety of schools
6. Length of experience
7. Good relations with staff
8. Subject specialism

9. Administrative ability
10. Extra-curricular work
11. Strong personality
12. Course attendance
13. Outside experience

Professional Development

Given this high degree of professional consensus, how can teachers prepare more adequately for promotion? The teachers resisted the type of 'objective appraisal' coupled with confidential reports, which is the basis of of the annual report of the civil service's hierarchical system of promotion, and similarly resisted attempts at performance appraisals[13] followed by some industrial organisations, with check lists related to job related behaviour. The roots of this resistance was the recognition that teaching was a highly individualised process depending on many variables − school environment, school organisations, resource availability, parental backing, LEA policies, calibre of head teachers, to mention only some − and that the risk of subjective performance appraisals as a major criterion for promotions are likely to make the existing, and often unsatisfactory position, even worse. The mood in the profession, and the moves by the employers, has been towards a planned and structured professional development, involving, at each stage, evaluation of performance, and an opportunity to discuss this with other professionals. What is needed is a proper system of career development; this would involve both individual class teachers and head teachers on a reciprocal and mutually acceptable basis, with frank and open discussion replacing the system of confidential reports. Indeed, in a good many schools, where the climate is one of openness, such a system already exists.

Every teacher should be entitled to an annual career development interview, evaluating not only his own performance with the head and other senior colleagues, but having the right to state views on the efficiency and character of the school organisation itself, and the related resource questions, since these clearly affect performance in the classroom. For such an exercise to be fruitful a written record would be needed. This should include both the teacher's view of himself, a senior colleague's view of the teacher, and also the teacher's view of the organisational setting in which he conducts his teaching. It should be related closely to a job specification to which each teacher should be entitled on taking up an appointment, and be based on firmly established professional criteria of the type listed in the NFER table. Such a record, created by all parties concerned, containing genuine professional views which may, or may not, coincide, and built up over a period of time, would be vastly superior to the kind of reports now in use. Whatever the deficiencies of our present society 'reporting' on other people is, fortunately, being successfully challenged, and in any case, suffers from the deficiencies already noted. A mutual reviewing of professional practice, based on a system of self-appraisal, an exchange of views on how far objectives are being achieved, what constraints or other factors prevent, or promote their achievement, would have much to commend it. Apart from providing a detailed, open statement of the teachers' individual contribution to a school it could also identify in-service needs and help in the creation of a properly organised system of in-service training, to replace the present chaotic, *ad hoc* state of affairs where LEAs, the DES, teachers' centres, private and public bodies hopefully, or sometimes hopelessly, provide a hit-and-miss mixture of provision, with no visible attempt on the party of anybody either to co-ordinate what is in existence, or at least to establish proper priorities. Yet, whenever teachers meet in groups, often in staff meetings, and discuss such needs, priorities emerge quickly and clearly because they are based on a detailed knowledge of school life. One of the worst problems the profession faces is that the locus of educational decision making is away from the school, and that the decision makers are frequently remote from its day-to-day life. This is not to denigrate the work of education officers and advisers, nor to suggest that elected councillors should not participate either in educational decision making at all. What is needed is a clear recognition of the limitations of a decision making process involving promotion, which, by its very nature, must be based on second and even third hand reports, written in secret, on hunches, on the grape vine, and sometimes on sheer prejudice. The system needs not only changing, but sweeping away; the best guarantee for high professional standards is to let everybody know what you are doing.

Indeed, teachers cannot avoid doing this anyway; the quality of their performance is evaluated every day, in every home, by many thousands of pupils in thousands of schools, by thousands of parents. The successful teacher is not only the most successful practitioner, but the greatest harmoniser. Sensitivity towards children on a day-to-day basis, firmness existing alongside tact and understanding, recognition of individual needs within the classroom and in the school situation, reasonable accessibility to parents, willingness and ability to explain methods, contents and approach, understanding the effects of home and social environment on the learning process – all these are the stock in trade of thousands of successful teachers. This is not to say that the profession does not have its black sheep, its 'four o'clock' types, its cynical, disillusioned and sometimes incompetent members. Their numbers, we venture to say, are smaller than the authors of the 'black papers' suggest. The most recent reports of the HMIs[14] make no serious criticism of the teaching force, but state specifically that the majority of teachers work hard and conscientiously. But if the black sheep, the incompetent, have survived for so long and cannot be moved, is not this itself an indication that the system needs overhauling? Sir Keith Joseph's recent strictures[15] on incompetent teachers and the need to get rid of them, is not only a meaningless generalisation, but is nothing except political polemic, taking its place among such pronouncements, soon to be forgotten, as one Secretary of State yields his place to another.

The professional teacher has a clear responsibility to work hard, to care about the children he teaches, to understand that he is there to provide a service to the parents and to the community which employs him, and to do his best, however difficult the circumstances in which he finds himself. The justification for the teachers' defence of educational standards, their involvement in union activities, which protect the children as well as the teachers, their outcry against the cuts, their resistance to attempted tyranny, and their advocacy of good schools must rest firmly on the professional commitment shown by the vast majority. Each teacher who thinks of promotion must display such commitment as a starting point of a process which forms part of career development, beginning immediately after qualification and ending with retirement; there is no doubt that given the opportunity, the profession will rise to the challenge of controlling both the appointment and the promotion process from within, rather than without.

Notes

1. 'Scales of Salaries for Teachers in Primary and Secondary Schools, England and Wales, 1979' (Burnham Report) (HMSO, London, 1979) Appendix II.

2. See Burnham Report, 1978, Appendix II.

3. See *Promotion and Careers in Teaching* – S. Hilsum and K.B. Start (NFER Publishing Co., Slough, 1974). *A Fair Way Forward* – NUT Memorandum on appointments, promotions and career development – (NUT, London, 1981).

4. Five LEA's — Newcastle, Clwyd, Lincolnshire, Nottinghamshire and Somerset are co-operating in a project relating teachers' absences to stress; the first stage started in April, 1982.

5. *Promotion and Career in Teaching*, S. Hilsum and K.B. Start (NFER Publishing Co., Slough, 1974).

6. The NUT Report for 1980 gives details of conferences and motions passed at the 1979 Conference.

7. NUT Appendix to Rules — Appendix I Professional Conduct Code, Rule 54, Annual Report for 1980, p. 32.

8. *Promotions and Careers in Teaching* — S. Hilsum and K.B. Start (NFER Publishing Co., Slough, 1974).

9. 'Promotion and the Woman Teacher' — NUT Research Project published jointly with the Equal Opportunities Commission, NUT, London, 1980.

10. NUT Presidential Address, 1918 — 'Promotion and the Woman Teacher', NUT, London, p. 55.

11. The Secondary Heads Association has long advocated the establishment of such in colleges — see 'Towards Coherence', SHA discussion document (SHA, London, March, 1982).

12. *Promotion and Careers in Teaching* — S. Hilsum and K.B. Start (NFER Publishing Co., Slough, 1974), p. 125.

13. The NUT survey *A Fair Way Forward* contains a detailed examination of promotion methods used in the Civil Service, in the Post Office and a major motor manufacturing company.

14. 'Primary Education in England'. A Survey by Her Majesty's Inspectors of Schools (HMSO, London, 1978). 'Aspects of Secondary Education in England'. A Survey by Her Majesty's Inspectors (HMSO, London, 1979).

15. Sir Keith Joseph's Speech to North of England Education Conferences, Leeds, January, 1982. 'We should be failing in our duty . . . if we keep ineffective teachers in the schools.'

6 ACCOUNTABILITY

James Callaghan is often commended, or condemned, for raising the issue of teachers' accountability to parents, to industry, to society at large in his Ruskin speech.[1] He said that the matter and purpose of education demanded public attention; that this was not only legitimate, because £6 billion was spent each year on education, but necessary, if the shortcomings of the schools were to be put right; he identified these as a general concern with basic standards, especially the three Rs, in the primary schools; the suitability, or otherwise, of the curriculum for older pupils in secondary schools; he asked that what was taught should be more relevant to the world of industry and commerce; and he bluntly told teachers to abandon what he saw as a professional monopoly in the whole business of teaching, and of running schools.

But whatever the fame of the Ruskin speech, there is nothing new in the advocacy of the accountability of teachers. The history of elementary education in this country is also the history of the persecution of both teachers and children by the paymasters of the education service and their agents. The brutality of the system of payment by results was introduced by Robert Lowe in 1861 with words which have a familiar ring more than a hundred years later:

> I cannot promise the house that this system will be an economical one, and I cannot promise that it will be an efficient one, but I can promise that it shall be either one or the other. If it is not cheap, it shall be efficient; if it is not efficient, it shall be cheap.[2]

No such alternatives are available today; what the most strident advocates of accountability want is not only both cheapness and efficiency, but also control both of the curriculum and the methodology of teaching. The Black Papers[2a] are little more than an attempted revival of the codes governing teaching in elementary schools a hundred years earlier. The moves towards a centralised curriculum, the abolition of a Schools Council widely representative of teachers, parents, employers, trade unionists, civil servants, all of whom are accountable to their interest groups, by the present Secretary of State, and its proposed replacement by two nominated councils – one for examinations and another for the curriculum – in a sense, abandons the notion of accountability of the education service as such, and substitutes for it direct control by central government. In that sense, the present policies are both clear and crude: if you have direct control, you cannot have accountability, for accountability implies the exercise of judgment and discretion, control simply means that you do what you are told. Thus, control of the educational process, and the accountability of teachers to the various interest groups, are incompatible. It is this incompatability which is at the root of the great controversy.

This chapter confines itself to the issue of the school teachers' accountability to parents, and to the users of the schools' products in the post-school world, to further and higher education, to the world of work, to governors of schools, and to society generally. The accountability of the eduation service as a whole, that of the Department of Education and Science to parliament, is not dealt with, though it ought to be, in another book, at another time. What should teachers be accountable for? To whom should they be accountable and how should this accountability function? What happens in practice and what ought to happen? The debate is complex, but need not be. The issues which require examination relate to standards of achievements in schools, to teaching methods adopted by teachers, to the content and structure of the school curriculum, and to the process of educational decision making – who should be involved, in what manner and to what extent.

Resistance, by teachers, to attempts to control them and their daily work, to moves to put the educational clock back a century, do not and should not mean that the profession rejects the notion that it should be accountable for what it does and how it does it. In its evidence[3] to the Education, Science and Arts Committee of the House of Commons on Secondary School Curriculum and Examinations, the NUT states:

> The teaching profession recognises that it is accountable to society, but implicit in that accountability is responsibility. While society has a clear right to indicate its expectations of schools and to communicate these expectations through participation in local government, governing bodies and other means, teachers cannot be held accountable if they are not allowed to exercise full responsibility over the content and method of their teaching.

In practice, teachers are accountable, continuously, in an everyday sense, above all to the children they teach, and to their parents. This first aspect of accountability is often overlooked in some of the erudite debates — indeed, it is both interesting and significant how little mention there is of the children as such in the Taylor Report, in the outpourings on the curriculum by governments of both political complexions in the last six years, and by educational pundits a long way from the schools. But the actual process of teaching happens in the classroom. In a day and an age where the teachers' authority is challenged as part of a changing social structure, the actual process of everyday teaching contains the practical application of accountability. Explaining to a class what is done, why it is done, answering questions, being ready, day after day, week after week, to present lessons which must justify what is taught, and how it is taught, talking to pupils about themselves, their work, and their relationship with teachers, all amounts to accountability. To the teacher in the classroom, the need to carry the class along, to gain the pupils' support, to maintain the essentials of order without recourse to authoritarianism, to achieve the results which the pupils themselves, and their parents expect, is a far more realistic approach to accountability than the external aspects of the whole business.

It is one of the curiosities of the educational system that debate about what happens, should or should not happen is conducted with considerable vigour and ferocity away from the classroom; often the ferocity is in proportion to the distance from the school; the greater it is, the louder the shouting about what teachers ought, and ought not to do. This is not so in medicine. It is recognised that what the doctor does, he does on the spot and he is answerable for it to the patient. But because education has acquired, more and more, a political dimension, it is used by politicians for their own ends. The focus of the accountability debate has shifted away from the teacher/pupil relationship to the wider arena, where it is easier to pontificate about those who actually do the job. But the essence of accountability is in that relationship and there can be no doubt, and no reservations, about the teachers' accountability to the child he teaches — what he says, how he says it, the work he sets, the quality of his marking, the comments made, the handling of behaviour difficulties, the encouragement given, the necessary checks and sometimes reprimands, indeed, the 'everydayness' of it all, are accountability in the professional sense. It is thus a continuous process, existing in every classroom in every school, every day. Teachers must not, and do not, shrink from it. In this sense, accountability, as expressed in high quality teaching, direct to pupils, counts far more than accountability in the external sense.

But it has to be recognised that more is demanded, certainly by those who control the purse strings, though not necessarily by whom they represent – the parents, but more of them in a moment. One of the big issues is accountability for standards of academic achievements. Here, there are those, already identified, who claim that standards are falling, compared with an earlier supposedly golden age, when everybody was highly literate, and copper plate handwriting was the hallmark of a good education. They have brought forward no evidence either of the existence of such a golden age or of falling standards as such. What needs to be taken more seriously is the need to achieve standards in schools which equip pupils to cope with the complexities of living in the twenty-first century. This immediately raises a whole host of issues: What standards of literacy and numeracy are needed, at various stages in the computer and television era? Is not the ability to discriminate between a diet of violence dished out daily on a television screen and a good play, or documentary, showing long established values of truth, goodness and concern for other human beings to be rated higher, than the acquisition of knowledge of the literature of the seventeenth century? No teacher has ever denied that children should speak, read and spell, or should handle numbers, to the best of their ability. It is not an issue which requires a lot of talk and investigation; it is universally accepted by teachers and taught.

Unfortunately, the investigators do not think so, and an issue is made of it in the form of the most elaborate examination and assessment system which exists in the civilised and literate world. Prior to the abolition of the eleven plus examination and the widespread introduction of comprehensive education, the monitoring of standards in primary schools was said to be carried out by the selection examinations – attainment tests in English and Mathematics were used alongside IQ tests, to select pupils for grammar school education. Whilst there is little doubt that the system had the effect of crippling the primary schools for half a century by forcing them into avid, formalised teaching, the system itself was never reliable. The design of the tests, on which distinguished reputations were made, the conditions under which the tests were taken, the outcome – often absurd in terms of who 'passed' and who didn't – the sheer irrelevance of the process to the business of living led to its disappearance, and teachers in primary schools ceased to be accountable for the number of grammar school places gained every year. The result was that the primary schools flourished, and have never looked back. Throughout the 1950s, until the early 1970s, the National Foundation of Educational Research (NFER) tested reading standards every four years; the conclusion reached on standards was capable of many interpretations – but it was agreed that the findings were inconclusive and the tests were dropped in 1972. The Bullock Committee[4] sensibly, suggested a programme of assessing performance by means of a light sample taken over a continuous period, and asked that new and relevant criteria be established for a definition of literacy. In mathematics, the National Foundation for Education Research, an independent body financed jointly by the Local Authorities and the Department of Education and Science, had already produced 'tests of attainment in Mathematics' (TAMS) responding to demands to monitor numeracy alongside literacy. Such developments were not entirely welcomed by the Department of Education and Science, which felt that it ought itself to take the lead in what seemed to be becoming a matter of national interest and concern.

Assessment of Performance Unit

In 1975, the DES created the Assessment of Performance Unit (APU), the government's chief instrument for monitoring standards in schools. Its monitoring functions were, however, to have a definite purpose, to seek out underachievement, as stated in its term of reference:

> to promote the development of methods of assessing and monitoring the achievements of children at school, and to seek to identify the evidence of underachievement.[5]

The APU is serviced by a high powered team of Her Majesty's Inspectors. Its first head, HMI Kaye, his successor, HMI Marjoram, and the present professional head, HMI Graham, are all widely respected by teachers, but have more recently been working alongside Senior Civil Servants with a non-educational background, particularly Jean Dawson, designated as the Administrative Head of the Unit. The HMIs are advised by groups of specialists in their subject areas, and a typical specialist group contains the researchers, staffs of colleges of education, inspectors, advisers and teachers. The latter, however, are a distinct minority. Thus the steering group which produced the first report on language performance in secondary schools,[6] consists of 17 people drawn from the following categories:

5 HMIs

2 LEA advisers/inspectors
2 Professional Researchers
5 University/College of Education staffs
3 Heads of Schools

No classroom teachers are included. The Steering Group is mathematics, responsible for the second report on mathematical development[7] with eleven members, is not significantly different:

4 HMIs
3 Researchers
1 LEA adviser
2 University/College staff
1 Head
1 Teaching head

Whilst teachers' liaison groups exist, and are convened on an *ad hoc* basis at local level once programmes are underway, both the direction of the whole operation of monitoring, the interpretation of the results, and the responsibilities for publicity rest with a team of educationists which includes only a small minority of people drawn from the schools, where the actual process of teaching takes place. To say this is not to denigrate the worthiness of those who serve on the groups, but simply to point to a glaring deficiency in the whole process of monitoring at national level. Whoever has heard of a team of medical researchers which does not include doctors? Whoever would set up a project on technology without technologists? It is one of the absurdities of the whole system that the teaching profession itself is either not deemed capable of having sufficient members worthy of inclusion, or, and this is of course, the reason, that the political balance of the group is heavily weighted in favour of non-school teachers. The real expert in education is seen as the person who works away from the classroom and the school.

The APU holds regular, though not frequent meetings of its Consultative Committee of some 35 members, chaired by a university don[8] and contains representatives of the local authorities, including some chief education offices, of University Departments of Education, of the NFER, of parents (two) and of the teaching profession. Here, the teachers fare somewhat better — there are eight of them present, representing the teachers' unions.[9] The Consultative Committee is informed of the programme and progress of the research, expresses its views, and is seen as a body of some distinction and expertise by the DES; but it has no power of decision making — it is, simply, consultative.

The actual output of the APU has not been marked by speed. In the first three years, it produced nothing at all; the first report on primary mathematics appeared in 1978, to be followed by reports on English language in secondary schools in 1979 and 1981, and science in 1980. A report on foreign language testing is expected in 1983. To date, seven reports, four on Mathematics in both primary and secondary schools, two on languages in primary and secondary schools, and one on Science in schools, have been produced. Testing has taken place annually, usually in the spring in primary schools, and in the autumn at secondary level. Tests are usually taken at 11 and 15 years of age in mathematics and English, and also at 13 in science. When testing begins in foreign languages, only one age group, the 13 year olds, will be tested.

But the APU has not confined its activities to the testing of conventional subject areas. Some of its staff clearly see it as their function to monitor the physical, personal and social development of pupils; its brief to do so is highly doubtful, and it is not surprising that it ran into considerable trouble with its own Consultative Committee when attempting to establish procedures to monitor personal and social development, including pupils' attitudes to political, moral and religious issues. It set up an exploratory group to design tests and questionnaires which the majority of Consultative Committee Members considered to be a gross invasion of privacy. After strong representations, particularly from the teachers[10] and the parents' representatives, the ideas were dropped.

Attempts to monitor physical development fared no better. An exploratory group to look at 'physical competence and motor development' argued that nationally developed instruments of assessment would be helpful to teachers by 'drawing attention to the inter-relationship of motor skills of all kinds across the curriculum'.[11] It did not, however, say how or why. Finally, the APU concluded that it should not proceed with the project, but that a discussion document should be published and the views of teachers and LEA's obtained.

There have been lengthy arguments and discussions as to whether or not independent schools should be included in the surveys: whether this or that sampling technique should be used (a recommendation to reduce the extent of sampling was strongly opposed by the NUT on the grounds that it would reduce the validity of the findings);[12] which background variables should or should not be included. The picture that emerges is that the APU is, somewhat desperately, trying to justify its existence. Its administrative head writes in a newly published News-letter: '. . . formal surveys are not enough . . . we need to provide a wide range of published material to meet the particular interests of different groups of readers'.[13] In the same Newsletter, the Chairman, John Dancy, justifies the work of the APU on political and pedagogic grounds, claiming that in the whole accountability debate, 'heat is steadily being replaced by light', and that 'the APU can claim a hand in the revival of teacher morale since its low ebb in 1977 and 1978'.[14] One wishes it were so! Teacher morale is at its lowest ebb in the early 1980s, because of the cuts in education, the attacks on teachers' jobs, the hostility of the government, the meanness of many LEAs — but the APU is not widely known among teachers, and its findings have cer-tainly had no drastic impact, as the Chairman himself admits; he goes on to argue the case for some testing in the humanities and the expressive arts. But why? Who would benefit from such an exercise? Who wants it to happen? Indeed, what has been the value, either to practising teachers, or to pupils or their parents, of the sophisticated and carefully documented reports in English and mathematics?

The objective of identifying underachievement, and actually getting LEAs to do something about it, has not been fulfilled. The Chairman himself states that the APU has 'scarcely made any progress' in this field. The reasons are not difficult to find. The APU has failed to make an impact on teachers and schools, because its whole stance has been inquisitional, judgmental and often, full of jargon; it has not gained the confidence of the teaching profession because it has not involved teachers in its decision making, because it has failed to harness the day-to-day knowledge of teachers, confining them to technical testing procedures, and seeking to assume an expertise which it cannot possess, because it functions away from where the essential task of teaching children takes place — in the classrooms. As matters stand, it is highly doubtful whether the money being spent is well spent. It would be cheaper, and lead to more reliable results, if groups of teachers were given the time and opportunity to meet in the localities to compare their experiences, to look at pupils' work in their respective schools, and to learn from each other, as they do in so many other spheres of work. But to foster such a development would mean a different APU, and this has to await a more enlightened era.

It has to be said that neither parents nor teachers would miss the APU, and its reports, if it should cease to exist. For the parent, accountability functions at school level and relates to his own child, and to the teachers who teach him. It is the personal dialogue with the teachers, taking place at thousands of parent/teacher interviews, conducted every day of every school year in thousands of schools up and down the country, about the progress and problems, hopes and aspirations of the individual child, which counts. There is thus a clear and close relationship between accessibility and accountability: the teacher must, and does, make himself available to the parent, to listen to the parent, to explain, to comment on the child's progress: such a dialogue has in it all the elements of true accountability; it has the quality of immediacy — teachers and parents talking together; it is about real persons, in real situations; it is a continuous process, as the child goes through the school. It means that the parent forms a judgment of the quality of teaching based on what the child does every day, how he progresses, on the teachers' attitudes and methodologies; similarly, the teacher forms a judgment of the parent, the degree of support given to the child, his interest in the school as a place which matters a great deal to the child, so that accountability is a reciprocal process; parents are accountable to teachers in the context of schooling, and teachers are clearly accountable to parents. At its best, it is a harmonious relationship, but even if it is not, it is only at the personal, individual level, that accountability really functions — the rest is a theoretical framework which can be useful as a comparator, but is not essential.

This is not to say that there should not be involvement of parents, either formally or informally, at school level, to aid and facilitate the process of accountability. The existence of thousands of parents on PTA Committees and meetings where they discuss everything from the curriculum to sex education, and obviously make their views known, are among the most positive developments in the educational process in this century; the PTA movement has not only lessened barriers between teachers and parents; it has often broken them down.

However, alongside such positive developments there are still schools where the role of parent-teacher bodies do not extend beyond fund raising, and where the approach to parental consultation is not as encouraging as it ought to be. If schools want the support of parents, they need to be receptive to constructive criticism, be ready to explain teaching processes, and ready to use school governors to strengthen the links between the school and the community. The successful functioning of thousands of schools, the undoubted support given by the vast majority of parents even when they are asked to pay twice over for education — for this is what it amounts to when parents pay for books, apparatus, equipment, by special money-raising efforts — stems, at least to some extent, the tide of the cuts; the resistance of parents whenever school closures are in the offing illustrates clearly the stark contrast between what happens in practice, and the arid theory of the accountability debate. It is a contrast clearly recognised in the Taylor Report, the most recent survey of school government.

The Taylor Report

The Taylor Committee was set up in 1975 by the Secretary of State for Education and Science to

> review the arrangements for the management and government of all maintained primary and secondary schools, including the composition and functioning of bodies of managers and governors and their relationship with local education authorities, with head teachers and staff of schools, with parents of pupils and with the local community at large.[15]

Its brief was a major review of how accountability works in practice in the sphere of school government. Its conclusions published in 1977, are positive, sane and reflect the good practice found in many schools.

First, there is the insistence that every school, however, large or small, should have its own governing body; that power on that body to be shared equally between those who have a stake in the school's success — head and staff, parents, the local community, and the local education authority, each component providing a quarter of the members. Next, there is the recommendation that the governors should be given the maximum possible power to run schools, and that their decisions should be effectively communicated to the local education authority. This is followed by recommendations that there should be 'substantial' teacher representation and 'suitable arrangements for consultation with teaching and non-teaching staff.' Parents are recommended to 'develop whatever form of organisation suits their particular schools', and governors are asked to ensure that the arrangements for parents to be 'informed, consulted, encouraged to associate and generally recognise as partners both collectively and individually'. On the curriculum, Taylor recommends that the governors should

(1) Establish the school's objectives.

(2) Share in the formation of the structure of learning, care and rules needed to achieve these objectives.

(3) Keep under constant review the school's success in achieving its objectives, and produce regularly formal appraisals of its performance.

(4) Have access, in its task, to the professional guidance of advisers and inspectors.

Other recommendations deal with the governors' responsibility for behaviour in school, their involvement in the school's finances, their powers relating to the appointment and dismissal of teachers, and to the admission, suspension and expulsion of pupils. There is a significant, final recommendation that all governors should undertake training for their tasks as soon as practicable.

In evaluating the role of school governors, teachers have to acknowledge that in the present political climate, the major political parties will seek to tighten their grip on schools. Many experienced school governors will resist such a trend, but will nevertheless, be sensitive to the feelings of their local parties which nominated them, and expect them to take note of party policies. There is an important difference between interfering with the day-to-day running of schools, which teachers are bound to resist, and the proper and legitimate expression of views of a sizeable sector of the electorate, to which teachers must listen. The two notions are not incompatible and many governing bodies have found the right balance between professional and political interests.

The essence of the Taylor recommendations is that they seek to decentralise school government, and thus, the process of accountability. The recommendations are based on the clear understanding that the process of education matters most at institutional level, and within the institution; what matters is the individual. Eric Midwinter puts it well: 'It (i.e., Taylor Report) asks that institutions essentially human should be governed with a human face . . . each part of the whole relies on the harmony of give and take . . .'[16]

There are, however, aspects of the Taylor recommendation which requires close scrutiny by the teaching profession. The NUT's commentary on the Report[17] is critical of the 'sweeping powers' given to governors over the curriculum, and points to the likely growth of a bureaucracy of governors if they were carried too far. It is cautious about too hasty legislation on disciplinary matters relating to pupils, and comes down in favour of leaving it to heads and school staff to retain day-to-day control of discipline. The same argument is advanced in favour of heads and teachers retaining responsibility for the general design of the school curriculum, its content and teaching methods. The Union warns of the consequences of inexperienced, non-professional governors becoming involved in the day-to-day running of schools, and in the business of appraising the performance of teachers. While agreeing that it is important for governors to gain an insight into the nature of school life, and the complexities of the teacher's job, it points to the unsettling effects which too many, and too frequent, visitors have on classes. It draws a clear distinction between trained governors and the teachers who actually do the job. Nor is the Union too happy with the Taylor notion to devolve formal responsibility between LEA and school; it sees the value of a direct relationship between the school, the LEA, its education officers and advisors.

The caution and criticisms, echoed by other teachers' organisations, need examination. There is, in some of the Taylor recommendations, an enthusiasm for governors' involvement in school life not backed up by practical considerations. The case for training governors, the opportunities for dealing with the documentation schools would need to provide, the impact of requent visits, the time to be found by heads and teachers to talk to governors on a day-to-day basis require an approach to staffing levels, both for teachers and ancillaries, which looks out of reach today. There is also the natural caution of the professionals towards too detailed an involvement by lay people in the business of running schools. The important point here is the need for parents to feel secure that the teacher knows his job, that their child is in the hands of an expert, that the expert has had pedagogic training and therefore knows what he is about.

But the teachers have no reservations about the greater participation of parents in the running of schools. The NUT, in its comments on Taylor, states that 'parents and teachers share the responsibility for the education of children', stresses the need for fostering strong and good relationships with parents, and advocates giving them a third of all places on governing bodies, compared with the quarter recommended by Taylor; the same proportion is recommended for the teachers. There is thus a clear acceptance of the teachers' accountability to parents, on the basis of a shared partnership; the Union argues that there is much to be said for reducing the influence of local politicians on governing bodies, and preventing the creation of barriers between parents and teachers by giving too much weight to 'other interests'.[18]

It is essential, in any debate on accountability, to keep a clear perspective as to who should be accountable to whom and why. Teachers owe parents not only professional commitment, but are accountable to them, directly for what they do with, or to, the individual child. At school level, this accountability is both to the individual parent, and to the collective body of parents of the children in a school. There is, however, no good reason why it should extend to all sorts of other bodies including political parties, who claim to speak on behalf of parents, but frequently do not. The standing of politicians with parents is not necessarily higher than that of teachers; there is usually no direct communication about the individual child with them, as there is with the teachers. It is for the politicians to demonstrate for whom they speak, rather than act on the assumption that they speak for parents, and against the teachers, as is so often the case. The political process rests on controversy, whereas the educational process requires harmony. What is needed is fewer political, including party political elements, in the accountability debate, and more opportunities to project nationally what is working so well in so many schools – the partnership between parents and teachers. There is, of course, a place for the organised body of parental interests: the Advisory Centre on Education, the National Confederation of Parent/Teacher Associations, are not only important sounding boards but sometimes strong, national lobbies, usually working with the organised body of teachers; but they would not see themselves as substitutes for strong local ties based on the schools themselves.

The notion of reciprocity as part of the accountability process is also inherent in the relationship between teachers and the post-school world. There has been a tendency, of late, to confront the world of work, the employers, with the world of schools. Callaghan's insistence that the curriculum should be 'relevant' to the world of work, and Sir Keith Joseph's most recent proposals that the new 17 plus examination should have a strong vocational bias[19] suggests that the schools should primarily, if not wholly, educate for the world of work, for what employers want. This is not so. First, because education ought to extend beyond vocational preparation though it should never disregard it, or to treat it with disdain, as some of the public schools, and old established grammar schools did. The schools must educate the whole person, and not part of a person. Secondly, the world of work is an uncertain place, and there is likely to be less and less work for most people. Thirdly, the employers themselves offer no consensus of what is required, and see the teachers' accountability to them in terms of ensuring that basic standards of literacy, numeracy, general knowledge are linked to positive notions of punctuality, good behaviour and doing a fair day's work for a fair day's pay — a message spelt out in thousands of secondary schools every day. But equally, the world of work is accountable to the young people themselves, and to the schools which educate them. It is as legitimate for an employer to be critical of a school in a locality which is falling down on its job, as he sees it — and if sometimes there is an element of exaggeration in castigating some schools for turning out illiterates, it is reasonable to ask for evidence — as it is for a school to castigate insensitive employers who fail to answer letters, devote five minutes to interviewing an applicant from a school whose hopes to get a job have reached an almost desperate level after waiting months. There are black sheep on both sides, and both sides are acccountable to each other. There exists no inalienable right for teachers to be protected from criticism, nor do they expect it. There is, similarly, no rule which prevents criticism the other way round.

The same is true of the relationship of schools with the higher and further education institutions. Both are accountable to each other in a very real, and these days, closely defined sense. The grade require-ments of universities in 'A' level terms, the UCCA reports written by heads, and senior teachers to university dons, the account schools give of themselves and their pupils, all add up to acountability in action, with teachers not only having to consider very carefully the nature of accountability, but also the action they must take if, as a result of their teaching, candidates fail to get degree places for which they should have been adequately prepared. Anyone who has ever handled sixth formers during the vital period of the run up to 'A' levels, and has seen them following the publication of 'A' level results, which determine whether or not they are able to take up their university or college places, under-stands what accountability is all about. But who is accountable to the young people of today who are adequately qualified to proceed to degree studies, but cannot do so because the number of places has been reduced drastically at a time when the largest number of sixth formers since the war are to be found in our schools and colleges? Whom can teachers, parents and students call to account for such a state of affairs? The politicians, once every five years, when chances have been missed, and hopes dashed? It is high time that the focus on accountability be shifted away from schools and teachers to the decision makers at central government level, and to the county and town halls — for it is there that the real power lies, power based on the control of resources, on the principles governing resource distribution; the youngsters of today have every right to ask politicians and senior administrators to account for their decisions.

Local Inspectors and Advisers

Inside the schools, a well-oiled system of checks and balances exists to ensure that teachers are accountable not only to parents, employers, and higher and further education interests, but to other professionals. Local advisors are in and out of schools, giving advice, promoting their ideas, and sometimes, transmitting good ideas and practices seen in one school to another. This vast network of the local advisory service is rather more than advisory — indeed, in a number of local education authorities, notably the Inner London Education Authority, the term 'inspector' rather than 'adviser' is used for senior personnel, making it quite clear that there is an inspectorial element, that the inspector calls the teacher to account, and makes a judgment on the quality of the work in the schools. It is not unusual for local inspectors, and sometimes advisers, to make written reports to the chief education officers, both on individual teachers, and on individual schools, and it is not necessarily the rule that such reports are shown to, or their existence even divulged, either to heads or to individual teachers. But the relationships between individual inspectors and advisers with individual schools, heads and teachers are as varied as the education service itself, ranging from an excellent understanding based on mutual respect of professionals, to judgmental stances and prejudices which sometimes sour the essence of the partnership. Certainly, the newly qualified teacher can never afford to disregard the local adviser, who is usually given a specific brief to guide the probationer through the first year of teaching. Nor is it unusual for the senior adviser and inspector of a local authority to have a powerful voice in the promotion stakes; there is considerable evidence that the existence of a local advisory or inspectorial service is another powerful instrument of calling teachers to account for what they do, and how they do it.

Her Majesty's Inspectors

The position of Her Majesty's Inspectors is different, as far as the individual teacher is concerned. HMI can advise, and indeed, report, either openly or secretly, but cannot call teachers to account, except that in the case of young teachers in their probationary year, the final

word as to whether or not the probationary period is completed satisfactorily could rest with HMI. Here, the HMI has no axe to grind, and
his role is thus impartial as he is not accountable to the local education
authority for what he says and does. So much for the individual
teacher, but not for the individual school. The general inspection of
a whole school, whereby a team of HMIs descend on a school for several
days, is fortunately being phased out; instead, one or two specialist
HMIs concentrate on certain subject areas, on aspects of the school's
work, and normally discuss their findings with the head and the
teachers concerned. In recent years, there have been fewer and fewer
complaints from teachers about general inspections, and the attitude of
individual HMIs; thus the practice of HMI's calling teachers and schools
to account is less and less of an issue. This has been helped by the high
degree of professionalism, and the sturdy independence, which the
inspectorate, under the enlightened leadership of the Senior Inspector,
Miss Sheila Browne, has displayed in recent years. The inspectorate is
not there to please the Secretary of State, and since Sheila Browne
has been at the helm, everybody, including a succession of Secretaries
of State, knows it. Whilst one may question particular aspects, or
certain interpretations of the work of schools in the two massive
surveys produced by HMIs,[20] there is no doubt that these are carefully
documented, free from bias, and professionally produced by competent
professionals. Nor have HMIs shirked their duty in reporting on the
impact of the cuts in education — their most recent report 'The Effects
of Local Authority Expenditure Policies on the Education Service in
England'[21] is an interesting and relevant example of accountability the
other way round — the HMIs, in pointing to the disastrous consequences of the cuts on staffing, purchase of books and equipment, state
of school premises, in-service training, the advisory services, non-teaching staffing, have produced a survey which clearly requires the central
and local government to account for what they do, or fail to do, at a
time of severe reductions in educational expenditure. There may be
scope, in the general presentation of the report, for more joint enter-
prises between schools and HMIs; it would be good to see documents
which contain not only the HMI's findings on a school, but the schools'
observations both on the findings and on the way the inspectors conducted their business, and on the criteria they used. This is another
example of the reciprocal approach to accountability; but by and
large, the teachers, and the HMIs, are agreed on their priorities: they
are not on the politics of the day, but on the desperate need to provide
sufficient resources to maintain at least the most essential features of a

downgraded and hard hit education service for the next decade.

The greatest need is thus for the political decision makers to be accountable for their management of resources, for their priorities to parents and teachers, who concern themselves with the welfare of children on a day-to-day basis, rather than for a continuation of the sterile and artificial debate on accountability which has been proceeding throughout the 1970s and led nowhere.

Notes

1. See Report of Callaghan's Ruskin Speech in *Times Educational Supplement* – 22 October 1976.

2. Robert Lowe's speech to the House of Commons, quoted in *Accountability in Education*, Tony Beder and Stuart Maclure (NFER Publishing Co., Slough, 1978), p. 101.

2a. (i) 'Fight for Education', Black Paper (edited by C.B. Cox and A.E. Dyson), *Critical Quarterly*, 1969.

(ii) 'The Crisis in Education', Black Paper, Cox and A.E. Dyson, *Critical Quarterly*, 1969.

(iii) 'The Fight for Education', Black Paper, 1975 edited by C.B. Cox and Rhodes Boyson), Dent, 1975.

(iv) Black Paper, 1977 (edited by C.B. Cox and Rhodes Boyson), Temple Smith, 1977.

3. Taken from NUT Evidence to Select Committee on Education, Science and Arts, NUT, Hamilton House, London, January, 1981.

4. See Bullock Report 'A Language for Life' (HMSO, London, 1975).

5. Terms of Reference of APU–DES (HMSO, London, 1975).

6. 'Language Performance in Schools' – Survey Report No. 1 by APU (HMSO, London, 1982).

7. 'Mathematical Development – Primary Schools Survey', Report No. 2 by APU (HMSO, London, 1981).

8. Until March 1982, Professor Supple of Nuffield College, Oxford; since then, John Dancy, Professor of Education at Exeter University, and previously Head of two public schools, Lancing College and Marlborough College.

9. The writer has been a member of the APU's Consultative Committee since 1975, representing the NUT.

10. The writer presented a paper to the APU Consultative Committee in 1980 to argue the case against monitoring personal and social development. Sir James Hamilton, the permanent Secretary of the DES, attended this meeting and replied to the criticisms.

11. See Notes by Heads of the APU to Consultative Committee – February, 1982.

12. See the NUT's evidence to APU, 10 December 1981.

13. See APU Newsletter, Spring 1982.

14. It is fair to state that Beta Schofield, a member of the Science Monitoring Team, demonstrates that efforts, specially in Science, are made to produce really representative results – see her letter to *Times Educational Supplement*, 29 October 1982, p. 15. Gordon Bond, a teacher member, speaks of the frustrations and considers that the APU has wasted money (Ibid.). In his address to the

Annual General Meeting of the National Foundation for Educational Research, held in London on 21 October 1982, Sir James Hamilton, permanent Secretary to the DES, was critical of the progress of the APU, indicating a likely change in ministerial attitudes.

15. Terms of Reference of Taylor Committee (HMSO, London, 1977).

16. See Eric Midwinter's letter to *Guardian*, 27 Sept. 1977.

17. 'Partnership in Education', NUT's Commentary on Taylor Report, NUT, London, May, 1978.

18. See Dr Roy's letters to *Guardian*, 20 June 1978 and 28 Nov. 1978. 'Keep politicians out of school' and 'Down to the brass tacks of partnership'.

19. See 'Examining at 17+', DES, May, 1982.

20. (i) 'Primary Education in England' – Survey by H.M. Inspector of Schools (HMSO, London, 1978).

(ii) 'Aspects of Secondary Education in England – A Survey by H.M. Inspectorate of Schools', (HMSO, London, 1979).

21. HMI's report in 1981 – submitted to Expenditures Steering Group (Education) of House of Commons. The reports are general and do not name individual authorities, but it has been possible to identify some of them.

7 THE ESSENCE OF PROFESSIONALISM

The crisis in the education service, and the attacks on teachers, and on teaching, calls not only for resistance by the organised body of teachers, but makes special demands on every teacher and every school. These demands can only be made by understanding the essence of professionalism — the need to justify professional freedom and self-determination by striving for the highest degree of competence and commitment, both at the individual and the institutional level. Simply shouting for more pay and better conditions of service, gets the teaching profession nowhere; organising resistance to educational cuts may stave off the worst, but in today's turbulent economical and political times, will not, by itself, change the climate of public opinion, which, in the final analysis, determines the kinds of political decisions which emerge. Advocacy for more resources, for freedom from political interference, resistance to external controls must go hand in hand with qualities of leadership by a teaching profession not only determined to resist attacks, but capable of showing, in every classroom, in every school, that teachers really care for children, and for the quality of education for which they are responsible. There is nothing incompatible in being a good trade unionist and a good professional teacher. Both are part of the same process; the need is for teachers not only to protect their interests, but to identify these interests with those of the children they teach. This requires first a clear understanding that there is a strong, continuous and growing demand certainly by pupils and parents, but also by employers, by higher and further education interests, and the public at large, for high quality schooling. It is this demand which enables private schools not only to survive, but often, to flourish. What matters most to teachers in state schools are the attitudes of pupils and parents towards the teaching profession, for they, as the immediate consumers of the service, powerfully influence the climate of educational decision making.

The pupils shape their opinions almost entirely on the basis of what happens to them in school every day, how they are treated by their teachers, their successes and failures, and their conception of what school is all about. For them, each teacher they meet has his own, distinct reputation, depending on a multitude of factors, but not least, the teacher's professional skill, humanity and sense of humour. The parents are influenced by their own experiences at school, and inevitably make comparisons between that and what is happening today. Their image of the teaching profession is powerfully influenced by what happens to their own child in his particular school. The vast majority of parents come into contact with only a few schools during their child's school life: it may be as few as two, the primary and the seconddary school in the neighbourhood of the home. Thus, the judgment which parents make of the teaching profession is usually the judgment they make of the schools to which their children go, and this must inevitably be from a limited perspective based on meeting a couple of headteachers, and a small group of teachers with whom their children come into contact. Here, credibility is closely linked to the way the teacher does his job; how he speaks and dresses, the number of times he addresses an individual child, the extent to which he knows the ability, interests and the background of his pupils, the type of written work he sets, the frequency and thoroughness with which he marks written work, the way he communicates with the parents — all these contribute most powerfully to what is essentially a localised picture of the profession. As far as the parents are concerned, and they are a large, though not always an articulate group, there is no doubt that the credibility of the teachers depends not so much on what other people say about them, not on what is written in the local press, not on what they see on the television or hear on the radio, but on what actually happens to their own child, and what they themselves experience when visiting the school. This is not to say that other, sometimes hostile influences, are not present in parents' minds. But they matter less, and parents are often prepared to contradict them on the basis of what they see happening to their own children every day. To have a body of parents who speak well of the school, and who regard it as a good school, staffed by good teachers, is not only professionally rewarding, but is the greatest contribution which both the individual teacher and the school can make to the cause of education.

What then makes a good school? There are ten major components of quality as seen by parents and pupils:

1. High teaching skills in the classroom.
2. High quality pastoral care.
3. Speed and efficiency in communication.
4. Easily available, and easily understood information about the school and how it works.
5. School reports which are reasonably detailed and are issued at

regular intervals.

6. Availability and accessibility of teachers, including the head of the school.
7. High management skills as exercised by senior school personnel — heads, deputies, senior teachers.
8. Acceptable standards of tone and discipline.
9. Availability of opportunity to develop interests and aptitudes beyond the classroom.
10. Good educational standards, seen by parents and pupils as a curriculum containing the major school subjects, with some choice at the secondary stage, and good examination results.

The skills have been listed in an approximate order of importance, but they interrelate and determine the quality and ethos of the school.

The demand for quality in each of those areas manifests itself both at classroom and at school management level, and it is worthwhile looking at practical examples taken from successful schools which have gained a reputation for quality. Few schools are equally successful in all areas, and few parents expect perfection all round, but professional teachers need, and indeed, do strive, for the highest possible all round standard of their own schools. However, the concept of quality in schooling needs to be related, in the first instance, to those basic matters which are of major concern to pupils both in primary and secondary schools, particularly at the most sensitive point in their school careers, i.e. when entering a new school. Here is a list of what matters most to the children, both at primary and at secondary level:

1. How to get to school on time — involving coping with transport difficulties, unreliable buses, dangerous roads, and storing cycles safely at school.
2. Where to put one's things — safe storage of belongings, of books needed, of clothes, especially sports outfits.
3. Adjusting to the teachers — gauging the teachers personality, his requirements, and forming a good relationship.
4. Sorting out the timetable — where and when certain lessons take place, how to get to specialist rooms at the required time, with the required equipment and books.
5. Coping with learning difficulties — what to do and whom to see if something is not understood.
6. Making friends with other children.
7. Where and when to eat — understanding quickly how the school

dinner system works, what is allowed and what isn't in the way
of eating.

8. Understanding the system of assessments, rewards and punish-
ments.

9. How to meet homework requirements.

10. What to do in crisis situations arising either at school or at
home.

Teaching Skills

In the minds of children, the successful negotiating of situations arising
from the above list are as important as being successful in lessons —
indeed, success or failure on the classroom is heavily influenced and
sometimes determined by a child's ability to cope with the requirements of schools which are often, and inevitably, complex in their
organisation. Therefore, high teaching skills need to include not only
the ability to perform successfully in the classroom, but to understand
a child's needs at any given time. The willingness and ability on the part
of the teacher to deal with the 'chores' which often appear to have
nothing to do with teaching his subject, and the readiness to give firm
guidance when required, be it to the young child or to the adolescent,
are part of the equipment of the professional teacher. How then is
it possible to cope with the many demands made on the teacher?

Quality in human relationships means individual attention, and
those schools which provide an opportunity for each child to meet the
form teacher individually, regularly, though not necessarily frequently,
have achieved marked success. Individual attention here means not
only attending to individual needs in the learning process in the classroom, but developing a system whereby one-to-one contact takes place
outside the classroom. This can be done by instituting a system of
regular interviews, sometimes known as tutor interviews, whereby
school management makes available for every form teacher the equivalent of at least one teaching period each week, during which the teacher
is required to see three or four children successively on an individual
basis. The period is timetabled in the same way as a teaching period,
space being made available either in an office, or if this cannot be done,
in a classroom. In the course of short discussions extending over a year
or longer, the child gets to know the form teacher on a personal basis,
an opportunity exists to sort out, or at least to communicate, problems,
or for the teacher to spot them, which, with the best will in the world,

cannot be expected from her in the usual classroom situation, when 30 individuals may be demanding her attention.

This has the advantage that the teacher, being in a one-to-one situation with the individual pupil, is seen to exercise her professional skill for the individual, as is the case with doctors and lawyers, and not always in a group situation. This skill is shown to include expertise which goes beyond the classroom, and also acts as a constant reminder that she is a teacher of children, and not merely a teacher of subjects.

Secondary schools clearly find it easier, and certainly more necessary than primary schools, to arrange such interviews, providing school management is willing to give the necessary priority to the provision of this facility, for it is a question of priorities, even with inadequate staffing levels. Once the decision is taken that each form teacher shall have such a period allocated, the time saved in dealing with problems which may not be detected at all and then blow up, is considerable. During the interview period, simple documentation can be completed, on the basis of a simple questionnaire answered by the pupils earlier. Individual attention becomes a reality and not a slogan. It is one of the achievements of the best large comprehensive schools, that their very size has made them sufficiently sensitive to ensure that the individual is not submerged by the mass, that each pupil is always very well known to a group of teachers, though not necessarily to the head of the school.

Other components of the teaching process, for example, the involvement of pupils, quality in presenting lessons, the use of teaching aids, the setting of clear objectives, are the stock in trade of all successful teachers, but the setting and marking of written work often poses problems, because it is here that the dilemma of providing both quantity and quality presents itself most acutely. All pupils, including those at the infant stage, need to write regularly, though not necessarily at length, to achieve literacy. The secondary teacher specialising in the teaching of an academic subject may be faced with anything from six to nine classes, involving the markings of some 180 to 270 pieces of written work plus homework. This is a tremendous, and not always recognised, work load, which must be coped with, because pupils clearly expect their work to be marked and the attitude of parents towards the teacher and indeed, the school, is considerably influenced by the type of work set and frequently by the thoroughness of the marking, as well as by the systems of assessment used, and the comments made by the teacher. How to cope with all this is a major professional task. Useful procedures are to develop a system whereby not every error is marked, but to concentrate at various times, on different aspects of written work; the use of class rosters whereby marking of errors alternates with comments replacing detailed corrections, such comments being discussed between members of a class who will occasionally judge each others' work, is a technique frequently employed in mathematics lessons, but still to be developed in other subject areas: the setting of projects as part of a syllabus which leaves detailed marking until completion, a useful method evident in many primary schools, and in many CSE courses at secondary level is another approach. Constructive remarks are sometimes more useful than the continuous use of marks or grades, though these should not be excluded. Whatever the system, teaching skill, in the eyes of parents, is frequently judged by the way work is marked.

Pastoral Care

Pastoral care is an essential ingredient of schooling, but beyond the care and concern, which so many teachers show for their pupils in the course of their daily work, the need for a clearly set out and easily understood system of pastoral care, is increasingly being met in many schools, and is essential in large ones. The emergence of a careers structure in secondary schools recognises, and provides promotion for teachers to become departmental heads of subjects; but there has also emerged a system of appointing year tutors, heads of houses, group tutors, heads of lower, middle and upper schools where schools exist on split sites, in essence middle management staff working under the direction of heads and deputy heads. Many of the functions performed by these 'pastoral heads' are akin to those exercised by the head-teachers themselves, and it is one of the most positive features of large schools, that many more people, in addition to the head, are involved in decision making, in shaping school policies, and especially in overseeing the personal development, welfare and progress of each pupil, helping her to cope with the many problems which the complexities of modern life present to a young person.

An effective system of pastoral care allocates a group of children, either a whole year group, or part of such a group, if the school uses a horizontal structure (or a house[1] group if structured vertically) to one teacher, the year tutor, who clearly becomes identified with the pupils concerned. Hopefully, such a year tutor is given additional non-teaching time to have the opportunity to do a job as important as that of a

departmental subject head. Here again, the personal, one-to-one interview is essential for the diagnosis and remedy of difficulties, which will
often have been spotted by the form teacher in earlier interviews, but
who may not have the time to deal with other than simple problems,
and will therefore, refer them to the year tutor: thus, if a pupil has
difficulty in making friends, the year tutor speaks to all colleagues who
teach him, to other pupils in the group in order to bring about situations where the friendless one is spoken to, invited to participate in an
activity, given a task involving a group approach: such procedures,
whilst not difficult to operate, nevertheless need time and thought to
be set up. Once this has happened, and a friendless child finds contacts,
it can make a tremendous difference both to his own happiness and
indeed, to that of a whole family. In large schools, the compilation and
circulation of 'welfare lists' identifying pupils in need of particular
help, because of physical or environmental difficulties, and suggesting
remedies, as well as monitoring systematically what is being achieved,
can provided real quality in education.

But it is at crisis times when the pastoral system needs to be most
effective: when a home breaks up, when unemployment, sickness or
death affect a family, it inevitably falls to the teaching profession to
cope with the child showing day-to-day symptoms of stress. An essential measure in such situations, is to see the child individually as soon
as possible, and during the period of stress, frequently, though not
necessarily for long periods; to inform all staff who teach him that
there is a crisis situation, and so intervene decisively at crisis point to
enable the young person to cope with what is happening. Schools which
have systematically tackled the task of identifying such difficulties, of
informing all teachers concerned that they exist, and suggesting how to
deal with them, have achieved outstanding results, including reductions
in truancy, in delinquency rates – achievements which do not make
the headlines, but are more than worthwhile. Inevitably, lack of staff
and lack of time impose limitations on any system of pastoral care,
but where there is a well organised system, a great deal can be achieved
even with limited resources, given the knowledge and the will.

Efficient Communications

The effective functioning of a school depends to a considerable extent
on the speed, quality and efficiency of its communications, both within
its walls and with the outside world. Internal systems of communication,

whereby the informal and close contacts teachers have in staff rooms, are usually supplemented by regular staff meetings, departmental meetings, conferences, and appropriate feedbacks to senior staff, are well established in most schools. The large comprehensives have charted the way to a new approach to school management, recognising that a system of planned regular meetings is essential to shape school policy, to create consensus and to carry out what has been agreed — a long way from the 'captain of the ship' philosophy, whereby one person, the head teacher, conceived a policy, gave orders and saw that they were carried out. There has been a tremendous democratisation in the running of schools in the last couple of decades, which, although not well publicised, has led to a 'spread' in the decision making process, and to much better internal communication. It has been less easy to achieve high quality communication with the outside world, largely because most teachers are in a classroom all day, and are not available in offices to answer telephones; most schools suffer from a deplorable lack of adequate clerical assistance, making it difficult to do the job the way it ought to be done, but there are, nevertheless, some procedures which have proved useful in organising effective communication systems.

A useful device is to ensure that all offices on the school premises, including that of the head and deputies, are never left empty, but always occupied by a member of staff. Heads, unlike many other office based executives, spend a considerable amount of time away from their rooms, directing and overseeing the activities of the school on the spot, being involved in meetings, and the same is true of deputies and other senior members of staff. The majority of heads of secondary schools spend between about a third to a half of their time out of their rooms, and their deputies certainly 50 per cent or more, since they usually have considerable teaching commitments, which they fulfill in classrooms. In primary schools, headteachers are more often to be found in the classroom than in the head's room. During such times, their offices stand empty; schools which have timetabled the use of office space by ensuring that members of staff, including junior staff, are made responsible, for limited periods, for answering telephone calls, for dealing with callers from within and without the school, have achieved a tremendous improvement in the quality of communication. People who telephone the schools speak to a teacher, instead of being told that the headteacher is not available. In many cases, the teacher concerned will be able to give the professional advice expected, or will, at least, initiate a procedure to deal with the matter. Personal callers, whilst not always being able to see the headteacher, will, nevertheless, be seen by a professional. The member of staff manning the school offices gains valuable experience in dealing with professional situations arising outside the classroom, and improves his understanding of the management process. Staff participation in the running of a school is essential to its success, because it helps to bridge the gap between management and shop floor, i.e. the classroom, which sometimes exists. Professional matters dealt with by junior staff in charge of the front office, thus form the basis of discussion between senior management and junior staff, improving the quality of communication between those making the decisions and those carrying them out, leading to a better understanding of each other's tasks and problems.

People who send their children to the independent schools, expect not only high quality teaching, and a great deal of individual attention for their offspring, but also look for opportunities to develop their interests and aptitudes outside the classroom. There are probably few people left alive who claim that the Battle of Waterloo was won on the playing fields of Eton, but the tradition of involvement in extra curricular activities, particularly in games, has not only been adopted by, but considerably extended in, the state schools of the 1980s. The range of such activities available, and the interests catered for in the average British state school, often stagger visitors from abroad. Every kind of sport, dramatic societies performing everything from Shakespeare to modern plays, thousands of school choirs, orchestras, windbands, and a diversity of groups catering for every conceivable interest, are found in all types of schools and in all parts of the country. These activities are as much part of the life of a school as the lessons taught, and parents have come to expect them, In judging the quality of schooling, the type and range of activities available usually play a significant part when parents and children choose a school. It is fair to say that when children do the choosing, which is increasingly the case as the system of parental choice is extended, the reputation of a soccer and netball team, the opportunity to play in an orchestra, to join a particular club, spell out quality for the young person. Every school prospectus, whether of an independent or a state school, lists its extra curricular activities and probably every teacher, at least sometime during her career, provides one or more activities out of school hours.

Information for Parents

Whilst the state schools usually lack the money to publish a glossy prospectus, the availability of suitable literature for both parents and pupils is a significant index of quality. What kind of published material is most useful and what achieves the best results for the school? It is not the arid publication of the 'school brochure' asked for in the 1981 Education Act,[2] and the publication of examination results, which can so often be misleading if presented in isolation. First, there is the letter of welcome to the new entrant. As soon as a child knows its new school, a letter welcoming it, by name, to the school community, is an excellent first contact. A similar, but separate letter to parents is equally useful; letters should be accompanied by two kinds of publications, one designed for the pupil and the other for the parent. A pamphlet, entitled 'Welcome to Hewett'[3] setting out the basic information required by pupils and another giving reasonably full details of the school's academic programme, its organisation and activities, aimed at parents, and entitled, say, 'Parent/Teacher Co-operation' should give a clear idea of the schools' objectives, methods and expectations. Above all, it needs to contain details of arrangements indicating when and where parents can meet teachers. The way the parent/teacher association works should be included. If there is no association, the means whereby parents are consulted should be stated. This type of literature, simply and attractively produced, initiates both parents and children ino the world of school; once contact is made, there is a further need for regular information.

The publication of a terminal newsletter, keeping parents informed of school affairs generally is much appreciated, but needs a reply slip to ensure that the publication reaches its destination, and does not remain in pupils' pockets. In secondary schools there is a need to explain what is happening at various stages; pupils choosing option subjects at the beginning of the fourth year, and the linking of these options with examination policy, needs to be explained and a publication issued at the end of the third year, is essential. Separate sixth form literature, giving a reasonably detailed account of the organisation of the sixth form, of 'A' level syllabuses and other courses available, including those for 'Open Sixth' students, all provide necessary links between school and home. Such publications give a picture of a well organised institution, sensitive to the need to communicate its objectives, policies and achievements to the world beyond school.

School Reports

However, what matters most to the parents and to the pupils is the individual school report. In primary schools, the half-yearly report, usually written on an individual sheet, or in a report book, provides a sufficient basis for informed discussion on individual progress; at secondary level, the 'cheque book system' of reporting has much to commend it. This consists of a number of separate report sheets, written by individual subject teachers with a summary made by the form or year tutor. The reports are then fastened together in a booklet which looks rather like a cheque book. The advantages of this system are considerable: the teachers write on single, individual sheets, without having to wait their turn as they must when a report book or single sheet is issued; they tend to write in greater detail, and usually independently, as the comments of colleagues are not seen when the report is written. This is much appreciated by both parents and pupils who feel that a more individual assessment is made for each teaching situation.

Once the reports are written and distributed, opportunities to discuss them are both necessary and desirable, and it is here that the accessibility and availability of the teaching staff, particularly the head and other senior staff, is of great importance. Some schools manage to co-ordinate the issue of school reports with the arrangements for parent/teacher interview evenings, so that reports can be brought by parents, who have had them a week or two previously, to the meetings. The pressure on teachers during parent/teacher interviews is often heavy, and an appointment system is therefore useful. This can easily be organised in secondary schools; pupils take home a letter of invitation to parents indicating the times at which particular teachers can be seen, the co-ordination of several appointments being carried out by the pupils themselves. The proper organisation of parent/teacher interview evenings is essential, although some waiting cannot be avoided — it is reasonable for a parent to give up one or two whole evenings when teachers are prepared to give us a series of evenings. In primary schools, the form teacher is always the most important person to be seen, and this simplifies the system; at secondary level, parents value the opportunity of meeting say five or six teachers, and so get a range of opinions about their child's progress.

However, even the most carefully organised system of parent/teacher interviews leaves long gaps between such meetings, and many parents need more frequent consultation with the teacher, or conversely, teachers themselves may wish to see parents on particular issues without waiting for the usual consultation evenings. Here the institution of a 'Parents Clinic' is a very useful device. In the writer's school, this operates on one weekday evening each week: three members of staff are available; these are usually senior or pastoral staff who attend on a roster basis, their names and dates of attendance being published in the newsletter. Parents are seen privately, on a one-to-one basis, like their children in the tutor interview period. Sometimes the demand for such an interview originates with the parents, and sometimes with the teacher. Parents may also turn up on an *ad hoc* basis, but preference is given to those who have made appointments, either by telephone, letter or through their child. Experience has shown that there are many parents who are unable or unwilling to attend the standard parent/ teacher interviews, but are nevertheless, prepared to meet teachers on an individual basis, away from group situations. At the 'Parents Clinic' parents who do not usually come to school, can be met, at least a few times during a child's career, and in schools operating this system, parent/teacher contact can be as high as 95 per cent.

And what of the teachers who run such a demanding system? Some, especially senior teaching staff, accept it as part of their professionalism — the giving of time beyond school hours is widely accepted as part of a teacher's professional life. Where there are difficulties, and a particularly heavy burden is inevitable, some compensatory time off during the day is not unreasonable. This is a well established practice in institutes of further education, but as yet, underdeveloped in schools, largely because of understaffing, but also because the concept is simply not built into the organisation of a school. But as most teachers are willing, and indeed, anxious to meet the parents, a carefully organised system can meet all reasonable parental demands for both availability and accessibility.

Management Skills

The demand for quality in education also manifests itself in an expectation that there should be quality in school management. Leadership by the head and by the senior personnel is expected, though parents are little interested in theories of school management, but look for competence on the part of those responsible, shown by their ability to give relevant information, to solve difficulties, and to be accountable for what goes on inside the schools. Heads of schools are no longer seen merely in the role of academic advisors, but clearly emerge as general managers of institutions often of considerable size and importance. Above all, it is for the heads, as managers, to create with their staff, an ordered framework for learning and living, which the vast majority of parents expect from the schools: parents certainly want their children to go to schools which are progressive, but not necessarily permissive, an important distinction. In evaluating whether there is a need for change, the timing of such change, whether it is in the curriculum, in teaching methodology or in organisation, requires a careful judgment, which needs to take account of the fact that parents are slower to respond to change than teachers, and therefore, the rate of both curriculum and methodology changes needs to be carefully controlled. Some changes in attitudes by parents are easily perceived. Thus, excessively rigid approaches to school uniform, regulations relating to hair styles, are less and less accepted by pupils in secondary schools or their parents, although the need for a school to have an identity remains. On the other hand, a 'free for all' is seldom acceptable, and many secondary schools, faced with the need to meet changing attitudes, opt for school attire rather than school uniform, offering a range of style and colours which increase as the pupils become older and move higher up the school. Parents usually support firm rules prohibiting smoking and drinking, and expect to send their children to an institution where a civilised way of life reflects what is acceptable in a good home. Schools, like homes, vary and reflect each other; the setting of standards, however, must not be compromised, although a school always needs to appraise realistically the environment from which it draws its pupils.

The most effective answer to the attack on teaching is to teach well; successful professional practices of the kind described are far more useful than theoretical discussions in creating parental and public support and good will. The move towards self-evaluation of performance, described in Chapter four, presents no difficulties for teachers, given the essential climate of reciprocity between school management and school staff. Some of the measures described will not, as yet, operate in every school; others, equally good or better, function up and down the country, but are often not widely known when they ought to be. No assessment procedures designed by experts, no testing programmes of local authorities, no reforms initiated by politicians, no ideas, however brilliant, thought up by the best brains in the best university training departments, can work in schools without the active co-operation of the teaching profession. The teachers themselves, by virtue of their training, their day-to-day practical experience, and their understanding of the children they teach and the parents they meet, are best fitted to carry out the necessary reforms. This was realised by a far sighted president of the Board of Education — Sir George Kekewich who, writing at the beginning of this century, dedicated his autobiography to the teaching profession; his words are as relevant and meaningful today as they were at the beginning of the century:

> They, (the teachers), have always fearlessly attacked all absurdities of our educational system, have never cringed before officialism, have stood for progress — never for apathy or reaction — have constantly and consistently used their powerful influence for the good of the child as well as of the teacher, and have been the mightiest lever of educational reform.[4]

Notes

1. The 'house system' derived from the public schools, was a feature of the early comprehensive schools; the majority now use a horizontal structure, based on the 'year group'.

2. The 1981 Education Act requires each school to publish basic information for parents, and secondary schools must publish their examination results.

3. The example is from the writer's own school; thousands of schools have well produced brochures.

4. Sir George Kekewich dedicated his autobiography to the NUT — see *The Teachers' Unions*, by W. Roy (Schoolmaster Publishing Company, London, 1968).

INDEX